IN MEMORIAM

JOHN CORIDEN LYONS

1901 - 1962

UNIVERSITY OF NORTH CAROLINA
STUDIES IN THE ROMANCE LANGUAGES AND LITERATURES
Number 48

VITAL D'AUDIGUIER AND THE EARLY
SEVENTEENTH-CENTURY FRENCH NOVEL

VITAL D'AUDIGUIER
AND
THE EARLY SEVENTEENTH-CENTURY FRENCH NOVEL

BY

FREDERICK WRIGHT VOGLER

CHAPEL HILL
THE UNIVERSITY OF NORTH CAROLINA PRESS

DEPÓSITO LEGAL: V. 716 — 1964

PRINTED IN SPAIN

ARTES GRÁFICAS SOLER, S. A. — VALENCIA — 1964

TABLE OF CONTENTS

	Page
Foreword ...	9

CHAPTER

		Page
I.	Introduction ...	11
II.	D'Audiguier's life, literary career, and posthumous reputation ...	18
III.	Traditional motifs, devices, and techniques ...	49
IV.	Reflections of contemporary life ...	66
V.	Characterization ...	85
VI.	Evolution of form and style ...	103
VII.	The publishing history of *Lysandre et Caliste* ...	117
VIII.	D'Audiguier's permanent literary significance ...	131

APPENDIX A

Plot summaries of d'Audiguier's novels ... 137

APPENDIX B

A consolidated bibliography of the publishing history of d'Audiguier's *Histoire trage-comique de nostre temps, sous les noms de Lysandre et de Caliste* ... 159

Bibliography ... 163

Petit Châtelet, Paris (*Lysandre et Caliste*, Livre VII)

FOREWORD

Among the once prominent but now obscure figures of early seventeenth-century French literature, Vital d'Audiguier was regarded by his contemporaries as an author, translator, and editor of considerable versatility in prose and poetry, fiction and nonfiction. Despite their initial success, however, his works have long since gravitated to the scholarly limbo reserved for the otherwise forgotten writings of secondary authors; they receive little more than occasional references in footnotes and bibliographies or perfunctory comments in erudite studies concerned chiefly with his better-remembered contemporaries.

It has not been my intention to set d'Audiguier up as a literary master hitherto overlooked among French authors of his day. To do so would be to ignore the conspicuous intellectual and stylistic limitations which contributed to the eclipse of his works by the more artistic prose and poetry offered by writers of the following generation. The real significance of d'Audiguier's prose fiction is twofold: its popularity showed it to be representative of the reading public's literary tastes at a particular moment in history; its varying mixture of traditional and contemporary materials provides an insight on the unstable concept of the novel during that period of literary and social transition. Either aspect in itself would justify undertaking this first study of d'Audiguier's five novels and their context.

In view of the limited availability of these novels in printed form or on microfilm, a set of brief plot summaries has been included as an appendix. Readers who might not otherwise have quick access to the texts will thus be able to note the context of the incidents, elements, or characters which are discussed in the course of this study.

The casual attitude exhibited by early seventeenth-century authors toward orthography —combined with frequent printer's errors— has resulted in many irregularities of spelling and consequently of grammar in the original texts. Apart from the changing of *i* and *u* (when used as consonants) to *j* and *v* and the substitution of *et* for the ampersand symbol, no attempt has been made in this study to regularize spelling, grammar, or the use of diacritical marks. Quotations have been reproduced as they appear in the texts.

It is with considerable gratitude that I take this opportunity to thank Professor J. C. Lyons of the University of North Carolina Department of Romance Languages for his interest and patience in directing the preparation of this study as a doctoral dissertation. I also wish to thank Professor John E. Keller, Professor Alfred G. Engstrom, and my former colleague James Waring McCrady for their helpful and timely suggestions. I am greatly indebted to Miss Louise McG. Hall and her staff of the University of North Carolina Library Humanities Division and to Mrs. Eva McKenna, formerly chief of its Interlibrary Center, for locating and obtaining for me many of the most important bibliographical sources used in this study.

Chapter I

INTRODUCTION

Scholarly appreciation of early seventeenth-century French fiction is a surprisingly recent phenomenon. The relative indifference of the *Grand Siècle* to the theoretical side of this genre —a modern, flexible form not rooted in Ancient literary tradition— was followed by two centuries of concern for a few monuments of the seventeenth century, apparently regarded as the only novels of the period worth recalling, although perhaps not rereading.

During the seventeenth century itself, critics of prose fiction tended to be either scornful of it or apologetic and defensive if novelists themselves. Soon after Charles Sorel's early attack on the fictional traditions of hackneyed devices and affected language, the targets of his satirical *Berger extravagant* (1627), others attempted to legitimitize fiction by fusing it with the ancient and respectable genre of epic poetry, thereby endowing it with essentially the same rules and conventions which had governed the epic since the time of Aristotle.[1] But even this effort failed to win general critical approval for the novel from the standpoint of literary merit, despite the indisputable popularity of fiction in general and the novel in particular during the seventeenth century. Contaminated by a vague association with untruth, it continued to be ignored or else spoken of disdainfully as being inferior to its lately acquired foster-brother, the epic.[2]

---

[1] See RENÉ BRAY, *La Formation de la doctrine classique en France* (Paris: Hachette, 1927), p. 347.

[2] Boileau's jibe in the *Art poétique* is probably representative of this attitude: "Dans un Roman frivole aisément tout s'excuse. / C'est assez qu'en

In addition to being frowned upon for artistic deficiencies, prose fiction was a constant target for ecclesiastical criticism on moral grounds. Recognition of its potentialities as a worthwhile literary form began to occur only in the 1670's and did not become general until the second quarter of the next century.[3] Its first modern advocate of note in the late seventeenth century was a prominent clergyman, Bishop Huet, who retained enough of the old prejudice against it in his brief history of fiction to observe that novels constitute an "agréable amusement des honnêtes paresseux".[4] After discussing the alleged corruption of women's literary judgment as a result of their preference of novels to more serious reading in recent years, he comments, "Ainsi, une bonne cause a produit un très-mauvais effet; et la beauté de nos romans a attiré le mépris de belles lettres, et ensuite l'ignorance."[5] Attempting to mitigate this emphatic statement, he adds rather lamely, "Je ne prétends pas pour cela en condamner la lecture. Les meilleures choses du monde ont toujours quelques suites fâcheuses."[6] Even the enthusiastic conclusion of his essay seems to justify fiction only on the basis of a secondary and unconvincing utility:

> Ajoutons...que rien ne dérouille tant l'esprit, ne sert tant à le façonner et le rendre propre au monde que la lecture des bons romans. Ce sont des précepteurs muets, qui succèdent à ceux du collège, et qui apprennent à parler et à vivre d'une méthode bien plus instructive et bien plus persuasive que la leur, et de qui on peut dire...qu'elle enseigne la morale plus fortement et mieux que les philosophes les plus habiles.[7]

The good standing achieved by the post-Classical novel in the eighteenth century was not accompanied by a critical rehabilita-

---

courant la fiction amuse; / Trop de rigueur alors serait hors de raison". (Chant III, 11. 119-121.)

[3] See Moses Ratner, *Theory and Criticism of the Novel in France from the "Astrée" to 1750* (New York: De Palma, 1938), pp. 5 ff.

[4] Pierre-Daniel Huet, "De l'origine des romans", in Marie-Madeleine de la Vergne, comtesse de La Fayette, *Oeuvres* (Paris: Garnier Frères, 1864), p. 465.

[5] *Ibid.*, p. 508.

[6] *Ibid.*

[7] *Ibid.*, p. 509.

tion of its seventeenth-century counterpart. In view of the persistent general disregard for irregular works unblessed by Boileau and his fellow legislators of literary propriety, there could be little incentive to trace the evolution of the novel from the Renaissance concept of prose fiction still in evidence in 1600 to the modern psychological analysis of *La Princesse de Clèves* toward the end of the century.

It is somewhat ironic that the first major literary historian to examine that evolution should be an Englishman. In his early nineteenth-century *History of Fiction*, J. C. Dunlop links d'Urfé's *Astrée*, the *roman comique*, and the later *romans de longue haleine* of Gomberville, La Calprenède, and the Scudérys to their Italian and Spanish prototypes with fair accuracy before proceeding to discuss Madame de La Fayette. [8] What he fails to observe, however, is a transitional period of assimilation and adaptation during the late sixteenth and early seventeenth centuries; it was then that the actual groundwork was laid for the French works which he describes.

Between 1857 and 1862, Louis de Loménie published a series of articles reviewing the development of prose fiction in France through the reign of Louis XIII. Although well written, these articles reveal the same flaw seen in Dunlop's study, for de Loménie neglects the many other novels appearing during that transitional period in which the first three parts of the *Astrée* constitute an isolated masterpiece. [9]

---

[8] See JOHN COLIN DUNLOP, *The History of Fiction: Being a Critical Account of the Most Celebrated Prose Works of Fiction from the Earliest Greek Romances to the Novels of the Present Age* (3rd ed.; London: 1845), chaps. IX-XIII.

[9] See LOUIS DE LOMÉNIE, "La Littérature romanesque: I. Du roman en France jùsqu'à l'Astrée", *Revue des Deux-Mondes*, 1er décembre 1857, 593-633; II. L'Astrée et le roman pastoral", *Revue des Deux-Mondes*, 15 juillet 1858, 446-480; III. Le Roman sous Louis XIII", *Revue des Deux-Mondes*, 1er février 1862, 722-749. A few years later, another literary historian did deplore the lack of modern research in regard to the neglected novels of the transitional period, referring specifically to those sold by the Parisian bookdealer Toussaint du Bray, who published most of d'Audiguier's works; see Charles Louandre, "Les Conteurs français au XVIIe siècle", *Revue des Deux-Mondes*, 1er mars 1874, 97.

In 1885-87, the German scholar Körting published a history of the seventeenth-century French novel, sincerely attempting to present a comprehensive study of the whole period. Despite the abundance of useful information contained in this work, it falls short of its goal. In addition to committing errors of fact (which suggest a lack of personal familiarity with some of the works he summarizes or discusses), he makes no real provision in his neat Germanic categories for the minor novelists whose works constitute the bulk of fictional production during the first third of the century.

Körting's history is nevertheless more valuable than corresponding studies by Le Breton and Morillot in the last decade of the nineteenth century. The latter does give his reader fair warning at the outset that there will be no probing into the substratum underlying the few well-known novels he chooses to discuss; in fact, he denies the existence of such a substratum:

> L'histoire du roman au XVIIe siècle est en somme assez simple. Quelque féconde et brillante qu'ait été la littérature romanesque à cette époque, elle n'a pas ce caractère de diversité extrême, on peut dire de confusion, qui rend l'étude du genre si difficile au XVIIIe et surtout au XIXe siècle. Elle tient tout entière, ou à peu près, dans cet espace de cinquante années qui va de la mort de Henri IV à l'avènement véritable de Louis XIV, de 1610 à 1660 environ; et les œuvres qu'elle a produites ne sont pas de celles dont il est malaisé de démêler les tendances ou de fixer les traits distinctifs. [10]

Having thus brushed aside any possibility of irksome complexity, he proceeds to make a categorical statement which shows no advance in fictional criticism since Bishop Huet two hundred years before:

> L'*Astrée* de d'Urfé est vraiment notre premier roman; elle est l'ancêtre, la source de tous les autres. [11]

---

[10] PAUL MORILLOT, *Le Roman en France depuis 1610 jusqu'à nos jours* (Paris: Masson, 1892), p. 1.
[11] *Ibid.* Cf. Huet, p. 509.

INTRODUCTION 15

It remained for two French scholars of the twentieth century to produce the first really comprehensive analyses of the multiple currents which characterize the early seventeenth-century novel. Gustave Reynier's *Le Roman sentimental en France avant l'Astrée* was the first competent discussion of the abundant transitional fiction which preceded d'Urfé's masterpiece and the later *grands romans*.[12] This monumental work was later supplemented with distinction by Maurice Magendie's *Le Roman français au XVIIe siècle, de l'Astrée au Grand Cyrus*,[13] an examination of the masterpieces and potboilers of French fiction in the period between 1620 and 1650.

These two works alone are enough to discredit the traditional restriction of critical attention to those isolated phenomena which have become the fictional landmarks of the period. Scholarship of this sort is typical of a new approach to the analysis of French literature through study in depth —the establishment of literary context— rather than the former tendency to literary hero-worship. The modern disinterring of long-neglected secondary authors and their works provides a much more accurate idea of the changes in a literate or semi-literate public's tastes and requirements over a continuous period than was possible through the nearly exclusive study of literary monuments. Traditional categories are discovered to be arbitrary and untenable in the face of substantial contradictory evidence, which can no longer be dismissed as the work of misfits — Lanson's "attardés et égarés".[14] There is no better example of this revaluation than the present recognition of something more than a literary no-man's-land between the age of the Pléiade and that of the *grands classiques* of the mid-seventeenth

---

[12] "M. Reynier a écrit ainsi un chapitre de notre histoire qui n'avait jamais été fait, et qui a son importance... Avec les deux volumes de M. Marsan et de M. Reynier, en y joignant le répertoire de M. Lachèvre, on atteindra le plus grand nombre des œuvres secondaires de pure littérature qui appartiennent à la période de transition entre la Renaissance et le siècle classique; on marchera avec plus d'assurance dans l'étude des chefs-d'œuvre; on aura de quoi les encadrer et les éclairer." (Gustave Lanson, "G. Reynier. *Le Roman sentimental avant l'Astrée* [compte rendu]", *Revue d'histoire littéraire de la France*, XVI [1909], 401.)

[13] Paris: E. Droz, 1932.

[14] GUSTAVE LANSON, *Histoire de la littérature française* (Paris: Hachette, 1920), pp. 366 ff.

century. The difficulty encountered in labelling it satisfactorily is largely a semantic problem; if "baroque" is ambiguous, some other term will do as well.[15]

The study of French prose fiction of this period has benefited greatly from the new outlook. By indicating works which though imperfect do correspond in many respects to the modern definition of "novel", this type of research has caused the point of origin of the modern French novel to be shifted in the thinking of most of its students from Madame de La Fayette's work to the sentimental fiction of the late sixteenth century.[16] One result has been that the relatively obscure novelists of the transition period mentioned earlier may now be identified as pioneers —however incompetent— directly associated with an important and flourishing genre of modern literature rather than as barbarous storytellers denied the grace to produce an *Astrée* or a *Princesse de Clèves*.

It is in this light that the career and fictional works of Vital d'Audiguier should be studied, for they have a significance which up to this point has never been adequately expressed. Even though the more expansive modern studies of seventeenth-century French literature seldom exclude d'Audiguier from at least footnote status, he has received only brief or indirect attention from literary historians except as the subject of one nearly useless biography written in the late nineteenth century. It is time for an examination of the form and content of his novels, as well as for the determination of their place in his own life and in the literary history of the period.

Although greatly hampered in his prose and poetry by undeniable limitations of taste and literary skill, d'Audiguier should be granted recognition for having won the esteem of many distinguished contemporaries as well as the attention of prominent detractors as an author of unusual literary versatility. It is certain that a number of his novels and translations were widely read, relatively speaking, a fact substantiated not only by contemporary references to them but also by the impressive publication of multiple editions at a time when bookdealers were already sensitive to the tastes of

---

[15] See GEOFFREY BRERETON, *An Introduction to the French Poets: Villon to the Present Day* (Fair Lawn, N. J.: Essential Books, Inc., 1957), pp. 47 ff.

[16] See F. C. GREEN, *French Novelists, Manners and Ideas, from the Renaissance to the Revolution* (New York: D. Appleton and Co., 1931), p. vi.

the reading (and book-buying) public. One such work of his, a long adventure novel first published in 1615, would fully justify his inclusion with honor among the successful novelists of modern times; for it became an international best-seller of sorts, appearing in five languages and some fifty editions over a period of nearly two hundred years.[17]

Despite early stylistic excesses on d'Audiguier's part, it will be seen in this study that he managed to achieve a relative detachment in his novels from the briefly popular affectations of language and style generally associated with the works of Nervèze and Des Escuteaux. His own vigorous personality was too strong — perhaps his sense of the ridiculous, also — to permit continued subjection to the vapid artificialities of his more notorious fellow novelists.

D'Audiguier's general lack of inventiveness is an important aspect of his novels, for they are truly representative of French prose fiction during the twenty years of his literary career. Beset by social and financial insecurity, dependent on the patronage of conservative publishers, he was seldom in a position to risk popular disapproval by attempting fictional originality. His novels reflect a conscientious effort to keep up with the tastes of a frivolous reading public through the selection of commercially acceptable motifs, situations, and even characterizations. Under these circumstances, d'Audiguier's once-popular work is an excellent index to literary standards of the period, which could not have been the case had he been more independent in his writing.

The abruptness and thoroughness of his literary eclipse within twenty years after his death is remarkable in view of the reputation he had previously acquired as a popular and esteemed novelist. Yet despite the artistic and intellectual shortcomings only too apparent in his works, a lack of literary merit was probably not the specific cause of their fading into popular oblivion and scholarly limbo. There is evidence that their decline was a rapid obsolescence resulting from a major change in French literary taste first apparent around 1630. The likelihood of d'Audiguier's having been the victim of a general movement toward literary refinement of thought and expression will be considered in the last chapter of this study.

---

[17] See Chapter VII.

CHAPTER II

D'AUDIGUIER'S LIFE, LITERARY CAREER, AND POSTHUMOUS REPUTATION

Those two convenient biographical landmarks, date of birth and place of birth, are not known with certainty in the life of Vital d'Audiguier, despite the candor with which he occasionally described his own childhood and family background. Of the approximate birth-dates ventured by later biographers, the most widely accepted appears to be the year 1569, based on Guillaume Colletet's statement that his friend d'Audiguier was approximately fifty-five years old at the time of his murder about 1624.[1] Likewise, no positive identification of his birthplace has been established as yet, the most likely guess being that of his nineteenth-century compatriot and biographer Ardenne de Tizac, whose tentative suggestion of Najac rather than its neighbor Villefranche in the Gascon district of Rouergue is apparently based in part on d'Audiguier's own mention of the venerability of his home city:

> Ceste cy est des plus vieilles, et tellement ancienne qu'on ne trouve plus rien de sa fondation; On sçait prou l'origine de ses voisines, mais sa naissance s'est perduë dans les rides de sa vieillesse...[2]

---

[1] A. A. BARBIER, *Examen critique et complément des dictionnaires les plus répandus depuis le Dictionnaire de Moréri, jusqu'à la Biographie universelle inclusivement* (Paris: Rey et Gravier, 1820), p. 56.

[2] VITAL D'AUDIGUIER, *La Philosophie Soldade* (Paris: T. du Bray, 1604), p. 14

Ardenne de Tizac also observes that the frequent appearance of the name d'Audiguier in the Najac town records as well as Vital's later known residence there would seem to justify choosing it as his probable birthplace.[3]

The family into which d'Audiguier was born appears to have been a good example of the impoverished but self-consciously respectable French provincial gentry so common in the inflationary economy of the later sixteenth and the seventeenth century. Lamenting his initial lack of opportunity to make headway in the world, d'Audiguier remarks that things might have been different:

> Or si Dieu m'eust faict naistre d'une bonne maison, eslevee au milieu de quelque grand'ville, cela est sans doute que j'estois du monde. Mais je suis nay d'une pauvre ville, d'une maison qui l'est encore d'avantage: et de parens qui valloient bien plus que moy, mais qui comme moy se sont si peu souciés d'eux, qu'ils n'ont laissé que ceste marque honnorable d'avoir esté gens de bien. Je parle depuis cinq cens ans, car mes geniteurs vivent encore, et c'est tout mon mieux.[4]

But he makes it clear that his family possessed a long and honorable tradition of noble prowess, effectively serving the King at home and abroad with the sword until military inactivity caused Vital's grandfather and father to enter the royal magistracy instead. He acknowledges the wisdom of this change under generally peaceful conditions but attributes his own preference for the military life to a strong atavistic impulse.[5]

His rearing and education appear to have been botched by well-meaning but negligent parents. Unlike Montaigne's carefully planned infancy, his was spent in the family kitchen as a page in the unedifying company of scullery boys. It was here, we are told, that he developed a precocious aversion to the academic life which was to make his formal education of little value, despite his father's ambition to have an erudite son and heir. Vital excuses this

---

[3] GEORGES ARDENNE DE TIZAC, *Etude historique et littéraire sur Vital d'Audiguier, sieur de la Menor* (Villefranche-en-Rouergue: P. Dufour, 1887), p. 4 f.
[4] Audiguier, p. 8 f.
[5] *Ibid.*, p. 20 f.

disappointing performance in part by criticizing the incompetence of his teachers in teaching the arts; how could he be expected to see their beauties if his teachers were blind to them?

> C'estoit de pauvres pedagogues qui n'en sçavoyent pas les Rudimens; que je hayssois par opinion avant les voir, et que je mesprisay tout aussi tost que je les eu veus. [6]

At any rate, his school years were wasted, he declares, leaving him worse off than when he started from an educational standpoint.

But, determined that his son should receive adequate training to succeed him as royal magistrate, his father sent him off "aux universités" — a plural necessitated by Vital's frequent shifting from one to another in the unfulfilled hope of finding a compatible school environment. Despite his father's Polonius-like farewell admonitions, Vital's prejudice against schools and his new-found independence combined with his being somewhat older than his classmates to result in hostility, insubordination, and a minimum of scholastic effort. Finally undertaking law studies as a filial duty, Vital promptly fell prey to "desbauche", which seems to have consisted primarily of continual quarreling and duelling even though he was subject to university discipline and without previous experience with weapons. Instead of creditable use of this ardor at the time in serving the embattled Henri III, he complains that he had become accustomed to "ribler les rues jusques à minuict, avec des dangers que je n'eusse pas courus à la guerre: où pensant acquerir quelque peu d'art, j'eus bien-tost perdu le bon naturel que j'avois". [7] By the time he was seventeen, Vital remarks, he had already engaged in seventeen duels:

> Ainsi n'ayant pas si tost apprises les Loix come violees, l'esclat et la beauté des armes finablement m'emporta. [8]

Having completed —or perhaps merely terminated— his formal education, the would-be swordsman returned in 1590 to Najac to

---

[6] *Ibid.*, p. 13.
[7] *Ibid.*, p. 133.
[8] *Ibid.*, p. 19.

assist his father in exercising the magistracy.[9] The usual dead calm of the region which he deplored was shattered in the following year by *Ligue* agitators attempting to stir up the bourgeoisie against Henri de Navarre. As an unswerving devotee of the new king, Vital was ambushed and seriously wounded by eleven men on February 26, 1591. On April 8, 1592, on his first outing after a year's convalescence, Vital and his father were again attacked and wounded by members of the same group.[10] Vital's impatience with law practice and with the isolation of Rouergue seems to have been made unbearable by the humiliation of these attacks, for ultimately he renounced his law career and his claim to the family's magistracy in order to seek a more gratifying occupation. Just when this event occurred is uncertain. It appears, however, that he remained in Najac long enough to earn a reputation as a dedicated and influential public servant; he is known to have been president of the Najac town council for several terms and an outspoken delegate to the Provincial Estates.[11]

His decision to leave home and abandon his hereditary career was by his own admission a severe blow to his family; he was the only son, and his only sister had become a nun.[12] But, determined to make a clean break, he commended his parents to an uncle's care and set out to the north with the idea of seeking his military fortune in Holland and then in Hungary.[13] His plan was promptly frustrated by an unscrupulous valet who absconded with the bulk of his master's resources as well as the better horse, a detail reminiscent of Marot's similar experience.[14] Making his way to Paris as best he could under the circumstances, d'Audiguier

---

[9] PHILIPPE-LOUIS JOLY, *Remarques critiques sur le Dictionnaire de Bayle* (Paris: E. Ganeau, 1752), p. 156.
[10] *Ibid.*
[11] ARDENNE DE TIZAC, pp. 125 and 135.
[12] CLAUDE-PIERRE GOUJET, *Bibliothèque françoise, ou, Histoire de la littérature françoise* (Paris: Mariette, 1740-1756), XIV, 341.
[13] An indication of French military activity in Hungary during this period (*ca.* 1599) is seen in Pierre de L'Estoile, "Mémoires pour servir à l'histoire de France et Journal de Henri III et de Henri IV", in "Collection complète des mémoires relatifs à l'histoire de France", ed. Claude B. Petitot (Paris: Foucault, 1819-29), XLVII (1ère série), 257.
[14] Cf. CLÉMENT MAROT, "Au roi, pour avoir été dérobé", in *Oeuvres*, ed. Georges Guiffrey (Vol. III; Paris: Morgand et Fatout, 1876), p. 182.

soon established contact with a number of eminent patrons at court, including Bassompierre and the dukes of Longueville and of Guise. As a *parvenu* hanger-on in the midst of Parisian high life, he seems quickly to have achieved the sort of existence previously denied him in the social backwash of Rouergue. Yet this new way of life proved to be precarious, for he reports long illness, continual duelling, financial ruin, and abandonment by his new friends; then came an equally abrupt recovery which wafted him "au faîte de la gloire". [15]

It was evidently at his point in his bid for worldly success that he joined the service and entourage of Marguerite de Valois, the estranged but not as yet divorced queen of Henri IV; at this time —approximately 1598 [16]— she was still in isolation with her own small court at the remote Gascon Château d'Usson. D'Audiguier's presence in her entourage around the turn of the century is well established, [17] but the date and specific circumstances of his partial withdrawal from it are still uncertain. Once divorced and at peace with her ex-husband, Marguerite came to Paris with her court in 1605 to live out the last ten years of her life as a cultural landmark of sorts. But although d'Audiguier continued to associate with Marguerite's salon after her arrival in Paris, it is almost certain that no later than 1604 a slanderous accusation —possibly in regard to some amorous misadventure— caused him to be arrested and confined in a dungeon for two weeks. His release was accomplished not by Marguerite but by François de Corneillan, Bishop of Rodez, a friend of the d'Audiguier family and one of his most esteemed patrons. Although he remained devoted to Marguerite until her death, crises like this imprisonment seem to have forced him to depend less on the regular support of patrons than on his own independent efforts to earn a living. It is noteworthy that his saleable literary production began at this time, an output soon to

---

[15] ARDENNE DE TIZAC, p. 17.
[16] *Ibid*.
[17] See in particular SIMONNE RATEL, "La Cour de la Reine Marguerite", *Revue du seizième siècle*, XI (1924), 1-29 and 193-207; XII (1925), 1-43. Also useful, although based largely on Ratel in regard to Marguerite's court, is L. Clark Keating, *Studies on the Literary Salon in France: 1550-1615*, Vol. XVI of "Harvard Studies in Romance Languages" (Cambridge: Harvard University Press, 1941).

achieve such volume and variety that his dependence on it as a livelihood is manifest, apart from artistic considerations.

Unfortunately, non-literary biographical details are not available for the period from 1604 to 1621. The sort of autobiographical comments found in his prefaces and in his works themselves are almost exclusively concerned with the penury and constant humiliation suffered by him as a gentleman-soldier turned *littérateur*. Fortunately at least one incident has been recorded involving him as a courtier of Marguerite, evidently at her Paris salon.[18] On one ill-starred occasion in her presence, he saw fit to denounce as worthless an outrageously flattering poem in honor of Marguerite by her madcap "poète crotté", Marc de Mailliet. Sure of her support, the offended Mailliet promptly recited an extemporaneous sonnet vilifying his critic:

> Excrement de Parnasse, erreur de la Nature,
> Seulement imparfaite en ce qu'elle t'a fait,
> ... ...
> Dieux! que c'est à l'oreille une triste avanture
> D'ouyr la voix qui sort d'un gosier tant infect...
> ... ...
> Hibou, pour ton foible œil je luis trop vivement,
> L'excez de ma lumiere est ton aveuglement...[19]

The ever-sensitive d'Audiguier was not satisfied with his immediate reply in kind, denying that he was an "excrement" but adding:

> Ce seroit morceau pour vous
> Si je l'estois d'avanture
> Un pourceau de sa nature
> Trouve les excrements doux.[20]

When Mailliet seemed to have been favored by the Queen in this dispute, d'Audiguier unwisely wrote a letter to her condemning Mailliet and expressing his amazement at her favor for such a man. For this indiscretion he was promptly banished for a time

---

[18] Ratel, XI, 26 ff.
[19] *Ibid.*, p. 27.
[20] *Ibid.*

but soon had the satisfaction of seeing Mailliet follow him into "exile". He gave poetic vent to his animosity in a comically libelous portrayal of Mailliet's vanity, ignorance, and cowardice, first published in 1606 as "La Mort de Souillard" and again in 1614 as "La Mort facecieuse de Maillard".

The last twenty years of his life were clearly a period of disillusionment as he struggled to retrieve some personal dignity from an existence marred by financial insecurity. In 1621, he did manage to realize a lifelong ambition by participating in Louis XIII's military campaign to reduce the Huguenot strongholds of Montauban and Clairac. This experience is reflected in his daily letters from the field to friends in Paris and in his later discourses criticizing the management of the expedition. [21] Nothing definite is known of his last years after his return to Paris until his violent death while gambling at the house of a magistrate's wife in 1624 or 1625, a brutal murder described by Colletet with admirable succinctness:

> On le fit jouer an piquet; on lui mécompta tant de fois son jeu, qu'il ne put s'empêcher de dire à celui qui le fourbait: *vous comptez mal*, parole qui fut relevée d'un dementi; et en même temps, plusieurs satellites, sortis de derrière une tapisserie, se jetèrent dessus lui; et quelque effort qu'il fit de parer leurs coups avec un escabeau qui lui servit quelque temps de bouclier et de plastron, il fallut qu'il cédât à la force, et ce d'autant plus que ses ennemis se saisirent d'abord de son épée qui était sur un lit. Il fut percé de plusieurs coups, et rendit ainsi l'esprit sous l'effort de ces tigres de qui la rage ne se put assouvir que par son dernier soupir; ce qui advint au faubourg Saint-Germain vers l'an 1624... [22]

It is Colletet again who has provided the extant contemporary description of d'Audiguier's personality and appearance in his mature years:

> Il était d'une taille haute et fière, d'un visage morne et mélancholique, et d'une humeur fort rêveuse et fort soli-

---

[21] Ardenne de Tizac, pp. 94-120 ("Le Critique historique").
[22] Guillaume Colletet, *Vies des poètes bordelais et périgourdins*, ed. Tamizey de Larroque (Paris: Claudin, 1873), p. 76 n.

taire; au reste, homme, sur la fin de ses jours, fort dévot et fort craignant Dieu, et toujours très-bon et très-fidèle ami.[23]

D'Audiguier himself indicated at the age of about thirty-five that he was unmarried and not in a position to win the only lady to whom he was devoted.[24] Although presumably an enthusiastic admirer of women, he remained a bachelor, frustrated by the conflict between his pride and his hand-to-mouth existence.[25] His vigorous and peculiarly tragic life has been considered by some modern critics to have been more colorful than the plot of any of his novels.[26]

* * *

From a literary standpoint, d'Audiguier's later career was anticipated early in life when as a schoolboy he was moved to write poems lamenting the unhappy divisions of a France torn by civil war.[27] More precocious still was his defiant poetical support of Henri III whenever ordered in school to compose poetry praising the *Ligue*; such independence at that time was liable to severe punishment by his wholly unappreciative Jesuit teachers.[28] His youthful devotion to Henri III resulted in the composition of a "Tombeau" upon the King's death in 1589. The twenty-year-old poet's allegory represented the late king by Achilles,

assassiné comme luy par l'infidelle Pâris, qui pour se mesler du different des Celestes, avoit encouru la hayne des Dieux.[29]

Likewise, French arms were symbolized by those of Achilles,

---

[23] Quoted in BARBIER, p. 56.
[24] AUDIGUIER, pp. 77 ff.
[25] GOUJET, p. 347.
[26] See GUSTAVE REYNIER, *Le Roman sentimental en France avant l'Astrée* (Paris: Armand Colin, 1908), p. 265, and Antoine Adam, *Histoire de la littérature française au XVIIe siècle* (Paris: Domat, 1948-56), I, 104 n.
[27] AUDIGUIER, p. 123.
[28] *Ibid.*
[29] *Ibid.*, p. 126 f.

toutes deux venuës du Ciel, toutes deux guerissans de maux incurables, et toutes deux causes de grandes querelles. [30]

His only extant writing from 1590 to 1604 is apparently found in political speeches prepared by him as a delegate from Najac to the Provincial Estates. Addressing the King, he deplores the precarious situation existing in the province, the unreliability of its supposed guardians, and the apathy of its inhabitants. [31] In 1602, according to a later remark of his, he prepared some sort of essay on duelling, a subject always prominent in his thinking and writing. [32]

In 1604, he began what may be considered his official literary career with the publication of two non-fictional prose works, *La Philosophie Soldade* and *Le Pourtrait du Monde*. The first, a handsome little volume set in conspicuously large type and with yawning margins, chiefly purports to be his stoical answer to his friends' nagging insistence that he strive more vigorously to get ahead in the world instead of remaining in unseemly idleness as a deactivated gentleman soldier. The second, substantially longer and hitherto a bibliographical mystery of uncertain genre, [33] was published simultaneously with *La Philosophie Soldade*. Sententious at times, shrill at others, it has the initial effect of a conventional sermon decrying the vanity and futility of human society but later assumes the form of something akin to an inordinately expanded Lenten devotion. Both works were issued by the Parisian bookseller Toussaint du Bray, one of the leading publishers of the day, [34] who was to be responsible for the printing of the majority of d'Audiguier's fiction, poetry, translations, and other works during the next twenty years.

---

[30] *Ibid.*, p. 127.
[31] ARDENNE DE TIZAC, p. 125 f.
[32] PIERRE AUBERT, "Bibliothèque du Richelet", *Le Dictionnaire françois de Pierre Richelet* (Paris: J. Estienne, 1728), I, xx.
[33] See FREDERICK W. VOGLER, "D'Audiguier's *Le Pourtrait du Monde*: Two Centuries of Bibliographical Confusion", *Romance Notes*, III (1961-62), 29-32.
[34] See FRÉDÉRIC LACHÈVRE, *Bibliographie des Recueils collectifs de poésies publiés de 1597 à 1700* (Paris: H. Leclerc, 1901-05), I, 46-69. See also David T. Pottinger, *The French Book Trade in the Ancien Régime: 1500-1791* (Cambridge: Harvard University Press, 1958), pp. 188 and 200.

D'Audiguier's first efforts as a novelist resulted in the publication of *La Flavie de la Menor* in 1606 and *Les Douces Affections de Lydamant et de Callyante* in 1607.[35] The first is a short prose epic based on the Francus legend concocted in the preceding century; this novel also contains a lengthy pastoral episode and a number of other typically sixteenth-century literary devices. The second is a short *roman d'aventures* in which d'Audiguier comes closest to conformity with the basically sentimental genre of the period, notorious for its affected language and threadbare characterization. In 1606 appeared his first collection of poetry, *La Défaite d'Amour*, as well as his edition of the poetic works of an obscure associate, Montgaillard, who had died in 1605.[36] Seven of d'Audiguier's poems were published the following year in the second volume of *Le Parnasse*.

In 1609, a collection of letters and essays appeared under the title *Epistres françoises et libres discours*; it was popular enough to be republished in 1610, 1611, and 1618. Of greater interest, though, is his modernized edition of Amyot's translation of Heliodorus; his revision was first published in 1609 and later reprinted in 1614, 1616, and 1626.[37] While not carefully executed —it smacks of the short-order publishing venture rather than of any disinterested scholarly concern— it is significant as a Malherbian effort to weed out archaic words and expressions and to regularize the often casual syntax of mid-sixteenth-century French prose.[38] His familiarity with Heliodorus is reflected in one of his own novels published six years later. Also appearing in 1609 was a reprinting of his "Réplique à Mailliet" in *Les Muses Gaillardes* as well as the inclusion of nine poems in du Bray's *Nouveau recueil des plus beaux vers de ce temps*.

---

[35] *La Flavie de la Menor* (Paris: T. du Bray, 1606); *Les Douces Affections de Lydamant et de Callyante* (Paris: T. du Bray, 1607).

[36] This edition is described in Goujet, XIV, 57 ff.

[37] See EDMOND HUGUET, *Quomodo Jacobi Amyot sermonem quidam d'Audiguier emendaverit* (Paris: P. Noizette, 1894).

[38] But Charles Sorel had praise for what he considered to be the remarkable purity and modernity of Amyot's language; see *L'Anti-Roman ou l'Histoire du berger Lysis, accompagnée de ses remarques* (2 vols.; Paris: T. du Bray, 1633), II, 933.

In 1611, his edition of the Maréchal de Biron's *Maximes et instructions de l'art de la guerre* was published by du Bray. This edition was doubtless a gratifying assignment for a man of d'Audiguier's temperament, frustrated warrior that he was.

In addition to the appearance of a selection of his poems in Esprit Aubert's *Marguerites poétiques* in 1613, he published a second poetry collection of his own in two parts in 1613 and 1614, retaining only a few poems from the 1606 edition. Significantly enough, while flattering more recent patrons like the Princesse de Conti, the author dedicated the second part of this collection to Queen Marguerite, asserting that all its poems were composed for her and were printed only by her order. Another grateful tribute to past patronage is seen in his ode on the death of the Bishop of Rodez in 1614, which was published in an anthology the following year.

The year 1615 was perhaps the most important in all of d'Audiguier's career, for it saw the publication of his two most successful works as a novelist and as a translator. In his novel, *Histoire trage-comique de nostre temps, sous les noms de Lysandre et de Caliste*,[39] over twice as long as any of his other novels, d'Audiguier somehow hit upon a formula which assured it an enduring popularity in France and abroad for the next 184 years, despite its many flaws of composition and content.[40] His other work of similar popularity that year was a translation of six of Cervantes' *Novelas exemplares*;[41] this was his wage-slave's share in an opportunistic

---

[39] The edition primarily used in the preparation of this study is Paris: Nicolas Gasse, 1633.

[40] The success of this book as a publishing venture will be discussed in Chapter VII.

[41] D'Audiguier's six are "L'Espagnolle Angloise", "Les Deux Pucelles" "La Cornélie", "L'Illustre Fregonne ou Servante", "Le trompeur Mariage" and "Le Colloque de Scipion et de Bergance". In his introductory remarks, after offering Cervantes mixed praise for inventiveness and fictional technique, he proceeds to disparage the lack of French "pureté" in Spanish fiction, attributing any Spanish superiority to borrowings from the Greek romances of Antiquity. "Ceux qui estiment tant leurs livres, ou bien ils sont du naturel des François qui font plus de cas des estrangers que d'eux mesme, ou bien ils n'y prennent pas garde: Ny moy mesme ne m'en estois pas encore advisé, jusques à ce que la traduction que j'en ay voulu faire m'y a fait regarder de plus pres. C'a esté la cause que je n'ay point traduict cestuy cy mot à mot, comme ceux qui pour acquerir la reputation d'entendre bien

publisher's hasty project to offer the first French translation of them, for the original Spanish edition had been published in 1613. Although d'Audiguier's lack of facility in Spanish forced him into numerous and flagrant infidelities to the original text, his set of *nouvelles* was apparently better received than that of his competent and scrupulous collaborator de Rosset, certainly an ironic commentary on the general reading public's disregard for scholarly merit as such. The joint work enjoyed eight editions during the course of the century until 1678 and was the basis for nearly all later French translations of the *Novelas* until 1775, in addition to exerting considerable influence abroad.[42] D'Audiguier's translation of Lope de Vega's *El Peregrino en su patria* (*Les Diverses Fortunes de Panfile et de Nise*) the previous year had been the occasion not only of his own first Spanish translation assignment but of the first French version of any work of Lope's as well.[43] Although the

---

l'Espagnol, font voir qu'ils n'entendent rien en leur propre langue. Je ne me suis point aussi dispensé de sortir de l'intention de l'Autheur, et pense avoir dit ce qu'il a voulu dire. Tellement qu'ayant gardé la nayfveté de ces conceptions, et embelly son langage; Je croy te donner ceste version plus nette, et par consequent meilleure que l'original..." (Vital d'Audiguier and François de Rosset, trans., *Les Nouvelles de Michel Cervantes* [Paris: Jean Richer, 1621], "Preface.")

[42] See GEORGE HAINSWORTH, Les *"Novelas exemplares" de Cervantes en France au XVIIe siècle*, Vol. XCV of "Bibliothèque de la Littérature comparée" (Paris: H. Champion, 1933). See also the bibliography indicated in Frédéric Lachèvre, *Les Recueils collectifs de poésies libres et satiriques publiés depuis 1600 jusqu'à la mort de Théophile (1626)*, Vol. IV of "Le Libertinage au XVIIe siècle (Paris: H. Champion, 1914), p. 149 f.

[43] See GEORGE HAINSWORTH, "Quelques notes sur la fortune de Lope de Vega en France (XVIIe siècle)", *Bulletin hispanique*, XXXIII (1931), 199-213. *Panfile et Nise* is incorrectly listed as one of d'Audiguier's original novels in R. C. Williams, *Bibliography of the Seventeenth-Century Novel in France* (New York: The Century Company, 1931), p. 7; the mistake was pointed out by F. P. Rolfe, "On the bibliography of 17th century prose fiction", *PMLA*, XLIX (1934), 1078. In this first translation of his, d'Audiguier promptly expresses his general opinion of the Spanish language and literature in characteristic terms: "Car generalement tous les Espagnols sont vains en leurs discours, impropres en leurs parolles, insolens en leurs figures, extravagans en leurs Conceptions, ennuyeux en leurs reditter, et si barbares en tous leurs escrits, que c'est presque un Galimathias perpetuel dont il est bien malaisé de se demesler. Tellement que qui s'amusera à suivre entierement leur Espagnol trouvera moyen de faire le sot en François". (Vital d'Audiguier, trans., *Les Diverses Fortunes de Panfile et de Nise. Où sont contenuës plusieurs Amoureuses et veritables histoires, tirees du pelerin en son pays de Lopé de Vega* [Paris: T. du Bray, 1614], "Preface".)

same edition was reissued with a slightly altered title ten years later,[44] it was by no means as popular as the *Nouvelles* of Cervantes or of some of his later translations. In addition to these major works, one new poem was published in du Bray's *Les Délices de la poésie* in 1615.

In 1617, d'Audiguier published *Le Vray et ancien usage des Duels*, partly an ethical study of duelling and the necessity of its effective but humane regulation, partly an historical survey of notable duels throughout French history. This substantial octavo volume of nearly six hundred pages was a sincere and characteristic gesture of concern on his part. As early as 1602, he had written on this subject, and the views expressed in *La Philosophie Soldade* of 1604 are essentially those of this later treatise. Bayle commends it as a book "qui n'est pas indigne des Bibliothéques". [45]

The following year, 1618, the Hispanophobe d'Audiguier's literary efforts were restricted to the translation of Spanish works, a task which he claimed to find highly distasteful. In the preface to his translation of *Marcos de Obregón* (*Les Relations de Marc d'Obregon*), he asserts that only an inexplicable vogue for Spanish works and his publishers' subsequent requests for translations have induced him to have anything to do with such pitiful works.[46] As Hainsworth observes,[47] these reasons must have been weighty in view of d'Audiguier's continued production of translations of conventional and picaresque Spanish fiction as well as of works of piety. Later that year appeared his translation of Cervantes' *Los trabajos de Persiles y Sigismunda* (*Les Travaux de Persiles et de Sigismonde*), a work which enjoyed at least two later editions as well as two reissues of the second edition; its final printing was undertaken in 1681.

Although authorized in November 1618, his more than 1100 page translation entitled *Traitté de la Conversion de la Magde-*

---

[44] Lachèvre, *Les Recueils collectifs*, p. 160.
[45] Pierre Bayle, *Dictionnaire historique et critique*, ed. Des Maiseaux (Amsterdam: P. Brunel, 1740-53), I, 381 n. D'Audiguier's work is listed in Carl A. Thimm, *A Complete Bibliography of Fencing and Duelling* (London and New York: John Lane, The Bodley Head, 1896), p. 20.
[46] Hainsworth, *Les "Novelas exemplares"*, p. 49.
[47] *Ibid.*

laine —based on a treatise by Malon de Chaide— appeared in 1619. His prefatory comments seem rancorous in such a work of piety:

> Je te donne icy à mon advis la meilleure piece que j'aye jamais traduite des Espagnols, et la derniere aussi que j'espere jamais de traduire. Elle est pleine de sçavoir, de devotion, et de curiosité, mais digerée à l'Espagnole, c'est à dire mal... [48]

The year 1620 saw only the publication of his *Stances en l'honneur de Louis XIII*, but the following year —despite his earlier wish to shun Spanish literature— there appeared his translation of Carlos García's *Desordenada codicia de los bienes agenos* (*L'Antiquité des larrons*). It was twice reprinted in French and twice in an English translation of d'Audiguier's work.

Although a single poem appearing in *Le Temple d'honneur* marked the year 1622 for him, he came forward again in 1623 with the translation of a bulky work of piety, the three-volume *Pratique de la perfection et des vertus chrestiennes et religieuses* from a work by Rodríguez.[49] In the same year, there appeared a sixteen-page pamphlet entitled *L'Espouvantable et prodigieuse apparition advenue à la personne de Jean Helias, laquay du Sieur Daudiguier, le premier jour de l'an 1623 au fauxbourg S. Germain. Ensemble la Conversion dudit Helias à la Religion Catholique.*[50] This work is apparently a short story or *récit*, thus d'Audiguier's first known published attempt at brief fiction.

In 1624, probably the year of his death, he was honored by the inclusion of several letters in La Serre's prose anthology entitled *Le Bouquet des plus belles fleurs de l'éloquence, cueilli dans les jardins des sieurs Du Perron, Coiffeteau, Du Vair, Bertaut, d'Urfé, Malherbe, Daudiguier, La Brosse, Du Rousset, La Serre.* D'Audiguier's last two works, *Les Diverses Affections de Minerve* and *Les Amours d'Aristandre et de Cléonice*, while appearing in

---

[48] *Ibid.*

[49] This work is attributed to him on Barbier's authority, even though it appears to be no longer extant. See Barbier, p. 57, and Hainsworth, *Les "Novelas exemplares"*, p. 248.

[50] This work is listed with a brief summary in the *Catalogue des livres composant la bibliothèque de feu M. le Baron James de Rothschild*, ed. Picot (Paris: Damascène Morgand, 1884-87), II, 266.

1625 and 1626 respectively, were probably composed in 1624; [51] the *privilège* for the former is dated May 2, 1624, and that of the latter, August 9, 1624, thus giving credence to Colletet's assertion that d'Audiguier's murder occurred about this time. Modern in setting and situations, *Les Diverses Affections* purports to be an autobiographical novel; in the "Advis au lecteur", d'Audiguier claims the authenticity of the events in this novel, excusing the possible reduction of interest for his readers as an inevitable effect of the narration of fact rather than fiction. [52] The novel is unfinished, breaking off at the end of Part I with the promise of better entertainment to come. What should be Part II is instead a separate work entitled *Epistres françoises et libres discours*, having only this title in common with the 1609 work; it is composed of a collection of letters exchanged between d'Audiguier and his mistress (addressed by a variety of names), a series of letters in Spanish between lover and beloved (certainly an unexpected effort on the part of an outspoken Hispanophobe), and a series of discourses primarily based on the 1621 campaigns. In the "Advis", the author ascribes his inclusion of the Spanish letters and the discourses solely to his beloved's express command. [53] This novel together with some of the French letters was published in an English translation in 1638. [54]

Aristandre et Cléonice is likewise very different from d'Audiguier's other prose fiction, for it is a frame novel with a setting of Louis XIII's court thinly disguised as that of the Sophy of Persia at an unspecified moment in history. Its rather meagre basic

---

[51] Although the first edition of the latter is usually given as Paris: R. Boutonné, 1626 (used in the preparation of this study), a 1625 edition is listed in Barbier, p. 57, and Maurice Magendie cites Paris: Gervais Alliot, 1624 ("Une 'source' inconnue du *Tartuffe*", *Revue des Deux-Mondes*, 15 juin 1929, 931).

[52] VITAL D'AUDIGUIER, *Les Diverses Affections de Minerve, Avec une apologie d'elle mesme. Et une Palynodie de l'autheur, et les epistres et libres discours du Sieur d'Audiguier* (Paris: Veuve M. Guillemot et M. Guillemot, 1625), "Advis au Lecteur".

[53] *Ibid.*

[54] VITAL D'AUDIGUIER, *Love and Valour: Celebrated in the person of the Author, by the name of Adraste. One part of the unfained story of Lisander and Caliste*. Out of the French by W. B[arwick]. (London: T. Harper for T. Slater, 1638).

plot of gallantry and intrigue at Court serves as a matrix for the narration of four long stories, which are of some interest as examples of brief fiction using relatively fresh or at least unfamiliar material. An indication of the topical basis of the main plot is seen in Charles Sorel's criticism of the artificiality of this type of novel; these *Amours,* he notes, "estans veritables, et n'ayans pas tant de diversité que des contes faits à plaisir, ont obligé l'Autheur à faire raconter une histoire à la fin de chaque livre". [55] Yet even this vigorous critic of d'Audiguier felt compelled to admit forty years later that this novel "n'estoit pas... des pires de son temps" — faint but significant praise from the Anti-Novelist. [56]

Although d'Audiguier's career does not lend itself readily to arbitrary categorizing by phases, it is possible to observe fluctuations in his choice of genres during the twenty years of his publishing career. To begin with, his non-fictional *Philosophie Soldade* of 1604 is solidly in the tradition of the unsystematic, unashamedly egocentric philosophizing of his Gascon predecessor Montaigne; candid and personal, this work propounds a similar blend of Stoic and Epicurean views with considerable recourse to Ancient examples and authorities. During the next two years, he turned to more conventional and probably more profitable genres: fiction, with two adventure novels bristling with traditionally popular motifs and in a style closer to the contemporary fictional standard than that of his later novels; poetry, representative of the forms and themes of the day; editorial work in preparing an edition of the poems of his late colleague Montgaillard. During the period from 1609 to 1614, d'Audiguier's work was primarily that of an essayist and poet, although his editorial ability was called upon in his modernized version of Amyot's Heliodorus translation and in his edition of Biron's treatise on warfare. His abandonment of the novel during this period seems remarkable in view of its continued popularity.

The period from 1615 to 1623 is doubtless the most important of his career. While continuing to write poetry and essays — for *Le Vray et ancien usage des Duels* is really a greatly expanded

---

[55] Sorel, *L'Anti-Roman,* II, 970.
[56] Charles Sorel, *La Bibliothèque françoise, ou le choix et l'examen des livres françois* (Paris: Par la Compagnie des libraires du Palais, 1664), p. 236.

version of earlier essays on that theme— he undertook Spanish-to-French translation as a major element of his livelihood. Without previous experience and without adequate training, he was bold enough —or desperate enough— to produce translations of some of the century's most important Spanish literature. His role as a translator has been reviewed in some detail by modern scholars,[57] but one aspect of his activity in particular is important enough to justify repetition here. Despite his apparent incompetence as a linguist and his wage-slave motivation in undertaking such projects, d'Audiguier did express an outlook on the process of translation which was to be the predominant view of the next generation of Classical "legislators", of Chapelain in particular. His position is essentially that translation is a base, inartistic imitation if faithful —word for word— to the original; it achieves artistic merit only if it manages to convert the original into a linguistic and stylistic form acceptable to the taste of one's compatriots, eliminating all that is irreducibly foreign to the reader's experience and speech.[58] This would be an alarming doctrine for anyone hoping to perceive a foreign author's style and expression even in translation, but nevertheless it is an important foreshadowing of the Classical principle requiring the reduction of literary thought and expression to the common denominator of seventeenth-century French polite society.

It was during this same important period that d'Audiguier achieved his greatest success as a novelist with *Lysandre et Caliste*, his first and last "roman de longue haleine". Unfortunately, the virtual helplessness of authors in dealing with their publishers at this time doubtless prevented him from enjoying a share in its financial success. There were no royalties in 1615, for an author was compelled to relinquish all rights to his book in an outright cash sale to the publisher.[59]

---

[57] In addition to Hainsworth, *Les "Novelas exemplares"*, see Esther J. Crooks, *The Influence of Cervantes in French in the 17th Century*, Vol. IV of "Johns Hopkins Studies in Romance Literatures and Languages" (Baltimore: Johns Hopkins Press, 1931) and Rolf Greifelt, "Die Übersetzungen des spanischen Schelmenromans in Frankreich im 17. Jahrhundert", *Romanische Forschungen*, L (1936), 51-84.

[58] See GREIFELT, p. 67.

[59] POTTINGER, p. 44. For a contemporary description of a Paris bookshop

The probable last year of his life, 1624, was marked by his return to the novel after nine years of writing in other literary forms. His two dissimilar novels, *Les Diverses Affections* and *Aristandre et Cléonice*, each reveal a departure from his previous adventure-novel concept. The first is realistic and even *comique*[60] in its bid for acceptance as an autobiographical account. As a frame novel, the second is most notable for its demonstration of d'Audiguier's efforts as a *conteur* rather than a novelist in his handling of the four short stories included. It should be noted again that his first work of brief fiction seems to have been the short *récit* about his lackey's miraculous conversion to Roman Catholicism, published the preceding year. Finally, in this same final year came d'Audiguier's last non-fictional prose — model correspondence and political-military essays in his new version of *Epistres françoises et libres discours*.

This summary makes it apparent that his career was characterized by a variety of genres and specific literary skills. It was not unusual for an author of the time to attempt a variety of literary forms in his bid for economic survival; surely d'Audiguier was as opportunistic in this regard as the next *auteur famélique*. Yet in this constant shifting, it is remarkable that he returns with new techniques to forms attempted earlier and then abandoned for years, as was the case with the novel.

* * *

During d'Audiguier's lifetime there arose an unflattering legend, trivial and suspect in its uncertain attribution, which has dogged his posthumous reputation ever since through its suggestive effect on casual biographers and critics. In his "Ode au feu Roy" (*Oeuvres Poëtiques*, 1614), he had excused his own deficiencies as a poet by pointing out his essentially military background:

> Que si je ne vole aussi haut
> Comme Du Perron et Bertaut,

---

and its stable of popular authors, see Charles Sorel, *La Vraie Histoire comique de Francion*, ed. Emile Colombey (Paris: Garnier Frères, 1909).

[60] The special significance as well as the ambiguity of this term in its seventeenth-century application is discussed in Adam, I, 134 f.

> Il faut pardonner à l'espee.
> Ma plume sent la qualité
> D'un homme qui porte au costé
> Le taillant dont elle est coupee. [61]

Describing this as a "bravade de Gascon", Sorel remarks,

> Il y en a qui asseurent que l'on luy repartit, que c'estoit donc à cause de cela qu'il escrivoit si mal: mais il ne faut pas estre di Satyrique. Il n'y a point de doute que cette façon de se vanter avoit beaucoup de grace, et qu'elle merite d'estre mise au rang des bons Apophtegmes François. [62]

In Tallemant des Réaux's version of this incident, d'Audiguier had made such a declaration verbally to Théophile de Viau, who then offered the crushing rejoinder indicated by Sorel. [63] Balzac appears to continue the legend in a sarcastic comment in *Socrate chrestien:*

> Nous avons veû à la Cour un Autheur de ce pays-là [voisin des Monts Pyrenées] qui se vantoit de tailler sa plume avec son épée: n'estoit-ce pas un vaillant Autheur? [64]

Aubert suggests [65] that Saint-Amant had this incident in mind without knowing the name of the author in question when around 1645 he composed his "Epigramme sur un escrivain de Gascogne", which is merely a rhymed version of the anecdote. [66] Aubert also observes that the last six lines of d'Audiguier's ode give a very different meaning to the poem, which was maliciously distorted by their suppression:

---

[61] VITAL D'AUDIGUIER, *Oeuvres Poëtiques* (Paris: T. du Bray, 1614), f. 10 A.

[62] SOREL, *L'Anti-Roman*, II, 960. This is transcribed without specific acknowledgement to Sorel in Bayle, p. 382.

[63] GÉDÉON TALLEMANT DES RÉAUX, *Historiettes*, ed. Georges Mongrédien (Paris: Garnier, 1932-34), VIII, 7.

[64] JEAN-LOUIS GUEZ DE BALZAC, *Socrate chrétien*, in *Oeuvres*, ed. L. Moreau (Paris: Lecoffre, 1854), II, 88.

[65] Aubert, p. xxi.

[66] See MARC-ANTOINE DE GÉRARD, (sieur de SAINT-AMANT), *Oeuvres complètes*, ed. Ch.-L. LIVET (Paris: Jannet, 1855), I, 470.

> Ainsi puissiez-vous, ô grand Roy,
> Voir par les effets de ma foy
> Le puissant desir qui m'allume
> De vous servir par le couteau,
> Et puis le remettre au fourreau
> Pour vous honorer par ma plume. [67]

A more convincing witness as to d'Audiguier's favorable appreciation by some of his contemporaries is seen in the frequent inclusion of his poetry in anthologies during his lifetime; Lachèvre lists eighteen of his poems which appeared in such *recueils* from 1609 to 1622, in addition to the inclusion of his poetry in still other collections of the period. [68] His prose was similarly honored in 1624 by the inclusion of selected letters in *Le Bouquet des plus belles fleurs de l'éloquence*. At about the same time, Guillaume Colletet included him as a notable poet and historian in a sonnet listing "les poëtes amis" and their talents. [69] D'Audiguier is in distinguished company here, for the list also includes Malherbe, d'Urfé, Racan, Boisrobert, Théophile, Maynard, and Saint-Amant, as well as several less familiar names.

In 1638, some fourteen years after d'Audiguier's death, Chapelain presented to the new Académie Française an ambitious project for the French dictionary contemplated since the founding of the group. [70] To establish this "trésor et... magasin des termes simples et des phrases reçues", Chapelain urged that a list be compiled of all the deceased authors who had written the purest French; the names selected would then be distributed among the Academicians, who would read the works of those assigned them and compile lists of "phrases et dictions"; from these, the Académie could swiftly select the whole body of the language and insert these passages in what would constitute a *dictionnaire des autorités*. Although this project was soon modified to have authorities cited only when needed to justify questionable inclusions, it is

---

[67] AUDIGUIER, *Oeuvres Poëtiques*, f. 10 A.
[68] LACHÈVRE, *Bibliographie des Recueils collectifs*, I, 158.
[69] *Ibid.*, 148.
[70] PAUL PELLISSON-FONTANIER AND PIERRE-JOSEPH D'OLIVET, *Histoire de l'Académie Française*, ed. Ch.—L. Livet (Paris: Didier, 1858), I, 102.

worth noting that d'Audiguier was included in the original list of twenty-seven prose writers of distinction.

This tardy honor and Bishop Camus' praise for him as a "bel esprit et fort belle plume" in 1643 [71] were evidently the last unmixed critical tributes ever paid him. Long before 1638, his literary reputation had come under fire, as is apparent in Sorel's outspoken criticism in *Le Berger extravagant* (later known as *L'Anti-Roman*), first published in 1627. In this interminable and laboriously comical indictment of all types of fiction from the Homeric epics down to French novels of the 1620's, Sorel has many unfavorable observations to make about d'Audiguier's ability and technique as a novelist. Although *Aristandre et Cléonice* is subjected to harsh criticism, it is primarily *Lysandre et Caliste* which sustains the brunt of Sorel's attack; he probably considered it more harmful in view of its more ambitious design and sustained popularity. D'Audiguier himself is quickly dispatched by Sorel:

> Je croy bien que Daudiguier avoit bon esprit mais c'estoit plustost un soldat qu'un homme d'estude... [72]

As for the language of *Lysandre et Caliste*, condemned earlier in Sorel's novel by one of the characters for its "force phrases Gasconnes",

> Il est vray aussi que le langage de ce Roman n'est pas si poly que l'on a cru; mais s'il a des mots de Gascon, j'en sçay qui sont encore plus estimez où l'on en trouve beaucoup aussi. Or sçachez que par usage nous appellons Gascon tout ce qui n'est pas purement François et qui a du barbarisme. [73]

Both novels are condemned for their lame plot organization and their abuse of fictional devices. This aspect of Sorel's criticism is particularly interesting, for it indicates those elements and details of d'Audiguier's fiction which seemed unseemly, illogical, or ridiculous to some observers as early as 1627. Nearly forty years

---

[71] HAINSWORTH, Les *"Novelas exemplares"*, p. 47.
[72] SOREL, *L'Anti-Roman*, II, 844.
[73] *Ibid.*, p. 967.

later, Sorel's judgment of d'Audiguier had mellowed appreciably in the *Bibliothèque françoise*. In his description of the lamentable state of French prose fiction at the beginning of the century, Sorel assails Nicolas de Montreux, Béroalde de Verville, and —most vigorously of all— Nervèze and his stylistic disciple Des Escuteaux ("dont le langage fut plus bigearre et plus monstrueux que le sien" [74]). But although only Gomberville, Colomby, Faret, and François Molière are praised as the earliest really good French prose stylists, d'Audiguier is mentioned sympathetically:

> Je ne pense pas qu'on doive mépriser absolument le sieur d'Audiguier...; Quoy qu'il n'eust pas beaucoup d'estude, il écrivoit en ce temps-là d'un style assez vigoureux et assez net, comme l'on voit dans plusieurs Romans qu'il a composez, dans ses Lettres et dans quelques Traductions. [75]

In regard to his language, belittled in the *Berger extravagant*,

> Au commencement ayant fait un Livre appellé *la Philosophie Soldade*, il avoit encore un peu de Gasconisme, mais il s'instruisit dans ses Traductions des *Nouvelles de Cervantes* et du Livre *de la Perfection de la vie Religieuse par Rodriguez*, de sorte qu'il pouvoit passer pour un de nos bons Traducteurs. [76]

Even *Lysandre et Caliste* is mildly referred to as an effort to provide a modern adventure novel, "bien commencée" despite its inclusion of unsuitable details. [77]

Sorel's discussion of d'Audiguier in the *Berger extravagant* and the *Bibliothèque françoise* is the only known systematic criticism of him and his work in the seventeenth century. That self-conscious prose expert, Jean-Louis Guez de Balzac, who must surely have had contact with d'Audiguier in Paris during the early 1620's, refers to him only once in speaking casually of an author at Court who had boasted of his military prowess. [78] Tallemant des Réaux

---

[74] SOREL, *La Bibliothèque françoise*, p. 231.
[75] *Ibid.*, p. 236.
[76] *Ibid.*
[77] *Ibid.*, p. 168.
[78] BALZAC, p. 88.

identifies him only as the author of *Lysandre et Caliste* in his version of the same incident.[79]

At the beginning of the eighteenth century, Pierre Bayle included an article on him in the *Dictionnaire historique et critique*, a distinction not granted Nervèze or Des Escuteaux—or even d'Audiguier's scrupulous fellow translator de Rosset. But times had changed for d'Audiguier's reputation since Chapelain and Camus:

> Auteur de plusieurs livres, qu'on lisoit beaucoup au tems de leur nouveauté, et qu'on ne lit plus aujourd'hui...[80]

Bayle reproduces several of Sorel's comments on the character and works of d'Audiguier. Much of the article is given over to an attempt to substantiate Bayle's opinion that d'Audiguier died in 1630; the basis for this idea is a letter by Balzac written in August of that year, in which he discusses the murder of an acquaintance in the Marais du Temple. Some of Balzac's remarks about the victim would be significant if they actually applied to d'Audiguier; this acquaintance is described as a spirited man whose principal fault was an unjustified esteem for his own literary merit, although "il n'y avoit point moyen de le souffrir parmi les Autheurs modernes, et dans le Recueil des Vers de ce temps".[81] Balzac mentions that this mediocre author died holding a grudge against him for having attempted to disabuse him about his literary ability. Although d'Audiguier is not named, Bayle is convinced that this is he, remarking, "Je crois que son caractere n'y est pas mal representé".[82]

In the unabridged "Bibliothèque du Richelet" printed only in the 1728 edition of Richelet's dictionary, Pierre Aubert included a three-column article on d'Audiguier, even though none of his works was used to provided examples for the dictionary itself.[83] Admitting that the prolific d'Audiguier was almost unknown in 1728, Aubert declares that he was nevertheless one of the good

---

[79] TALLEMANT DES RÉAUX, VIII, 7.
[80] BAYLE, p. 381.
[81] Quoted in BAYLE, p. 382 n.
[82] *Ibid.*
[83] AUBERT, pp. xx-xxii.

authors of his time in poetry, fiction, and translation, during a period when literary excellence was rare. Aubert discredits the vain-swashbuckler legend by reprinting the last lines of the unjustly notorious "Ode au feu Roy"; he then quotes passages from the *Oeuvres Poëtiques* of 1614 and from a letter included in La Serre's *Bouquet des plus belles fleurs de l'éloquence*. In the latter work, d'Audiguier declared his position on the relative merit of the pen and the sword:

> J'honore fort une belle plume... Mais la droite inclination de mon naturel, et la condition en laquelle Dieu m'a fait naître, me fait preferer une bonne espee. Je ne dispute point davantage des armes sur les lettres, ny des lettres sur les armes; Je parle de mon humeur, que m'a fait perdre plus de sang, courant apres des lauriers de Mars, que je n'ay jamais consommé d'ancre pour meriter celui d'Appollon... [84]

This statement is also used by Aubert to discredit Bayle's use of the 1630 Balzac letter to fix the date of d'Audiguier's murder. Aubert pints out the incompatibility of this statement with Balzac's description of a writer who discounted completely his own courage and military qualities, priding himself only on speaking and writing well. Moreover, Balzac's letter appears to describe an accidental death occurring in in a fight rather than an outright murder. Aubert believes that the problem can be resolved if qualified scholars are ever able to have access to Colletet's *Vie des poëtes françois*.

In his *Remarques critiques sur le dictionnaire de Bayle*, first published in 1748, Joly corrects Bayle's discussion of d'Audiguier in an article based so closely on Aubert's article that at times it is a word-for-word transcription — without acknowledgement. [85] After indicating some original bibliographical data, Joly dutifully echoes several of Aubert's sympathetic judgments as well as his speculation about the information hidden away in Colletet's manuscript.

---

[84] Quoted in AUBERT, p. xxii.
[85] JOLY, pp. 156-58.

The unavailability of Colletet's work hampered the Abbé Goujet's research as well, for he complains of having had to proceed without it, consulting when necessary the authors' original works in the Bibliothèque du Roi while preparing their biographies for his *Bibliothèque françoise*. [86] In the article on d'Audiguier, Goujet admits a substantial debt to Joly (hence, to Aubert as well) but offers much more biographical detail taken from material in the *Oeuvres Poëtiques* of 1606. [87] Like Joly, he dismisses the information provided by Sorel and Bayle as being inaccurate.

A surprising retrogression from the research of Aubert, Joly, and Goujet is seen in the article on d'Audiguier contained in the 1758-1759 edition of Moréri's dictionary, an edition incorporating earlier supplements by Goujet himself. Apart from some bibliographical information evidently taken from Aubert's article (including an incorrect identification of the first edition of *Lysandre et Caliste*), the article ignores all post-Bayle research on d'Audiguier, as can be seen in the following biographical summary:

> Vital d'Audiguier étoit noble et avoit servi long-temps dans les armées de France. Son humeur guerriere domine dans tous ses ecrits. Il fut assassiné on ne sait en quelle occasion ni en quelle annee: on croit que ce fut vers l'an 1630. [88]

Toward the end of the eighteenth century appeared two other historical-biographical dictionaries which gave his reputation short shrift. Dom Chaudon's *Nouveau Dictionnaire historique portatif* and the Abbé de Feller's *Dictionnaire historique* were later criticized by the better-informed A.-A. Barbier for treating d'Audiguier with unmerited disdain. [89]

In 1785, the *Bibliothèque des Romans* published a condensation of *Lysandre et Caliste*, preceded by an anonymous introduction offering a florid but not particularly informative account of d'Audiguier's career. [90] He is described as a man of strong char-

---

[86] GOUJET, IX, vif.
[87] *Ibid.*, XIV, 341 ff.
[88] LOUIS MORÉRI, *Le Grand Dictionnaire historique*, ed. Drouet (Paris: Les Libraires Associés, 1758-59), I, 500.
[89] BARBIER, p. 58.
[90] VITAL D'AUDIGUIER, "Histoire des amours de Lysandre et de Caliste"

acter and of imaginative and energetic artistic talent. Despite these qualities, the editor deplores d'Audiguier's vigorous, candid, excessively generous nature for having made him incapable of the coldly intellectual will needed to attain a good literary reputation.

> Tel fut ce d'Audiguier si inconnu, et l'on ne s'étonnera pas de son obscurité ni de ses malheurs. [91]

In an anachronistic slip, the editor asserts that Richelieu's Académie had decried d'Audiguier's style, which resulted in his not being invited to join it. The editor himself finds that style "assez riche, quoique peu soigné". He includes a list of several works by d'Audiguier with superficial comments, incorrectly attributes his "translation" of Heliodorus to a different, unrelated author of the same name, and repeats the discredited theory advanced by Bayle in regard to his death.

In 1820, a major contribution to d'Audiguier's biography and bibliography was made by Barbier in his *Examen critique et complément des dictionnaires les plus répandus*. This was made possible by his use of Colletet's manuscript, apparently sold by Pougens to the Bibliothèque du Louvre around 1808 and thus finally made available to scholars. [92] As a result of the destruction of Colletet's manuscript in the Bibliothèque du Louvre fire of 1871, Barbier's article has become especially valuable for its transcription of Colletet's well-informed discussion of d'Audiguier's career and murder.

As the nineteenth century progressed, brief conventional articles on d'Audiguier appeared in the important biographical dictionaries of Michaud and Hoefer. In 1887 came his first book-length biography, Ardenne de Tizac's *Etude historique et littéraire sur Vital d'Audiguier*, the work of a well-meaning but poorly equipped compatriot, who begins with the ominous dedication of "ces pre-

---

[condensation of *Lysandre et Caliste*], *Bibliothèque universelle des romans*, mars 1785, 3-10; hereafter referred to as *Bibliothèque universelle*.

[91] *Ibid.*, p. 5.

[92] Paul Bonnefon, "Contribution à un essai de restitution du manuscrit de Guillaume Colletet intitulé *Vie des poètes françois*", *Revue d'histoire littéraire de la France*, II (1895), 72.

miers écrits comme un témoignage de mon vif attachement au sol natal". [93] His attachment is never in doubt; his chapter on d'Audiguier's activity in Rouergue is perhaps his most interesting one, and his presentation of the early years at home is made up of lyrical paraphrases and amplifications of d'Audiguier's infrequent references to the subject. But Ardenne de Tizac's literary criticism wavers between an attempted rehabilitation of d'Audiguier as a poet of occasional equality with Malherbe, J.-B. Rousseau, and Millevoye, and a more modest claim for his recognition as an estimable second-rank poet, not among "les grands courtisans des Muses françaises". [94] Later comes a rueful admission that his unpolished style made him "nullement un aubain pour notre pays". [95] After long chapters made up primarily of quotations representative of d'Audiguier's work as a poet, moralist, and historian, Ardenne de Tizac declines to take up his role as a novelist because of the extensive background essay on seventeenth-century fiction this would require. Such an omission is astonishing in the biography of a writer traditionally considered to be primarily a novelist and serves further to invalidate the book as a useful scholarly tool. It is particularly galling that Ardenne de Tizac should then have proceeded to a sanctimonious and wholly irrelevant condemnation of Zola's naturalistic portrayal of love in his novels. What should have been a near-definitive biography becomes a highly subjective, incomplete, and unscholarly essay.

In 1894, in addition to his well-known doctoral thesis on Rabelais' syntax, Edmond Huguet presented a second thesis discussing d'Audiguier's revision of Amyot's translation of Heliodorus. The slight general interest in this subject that may have existed was probably largely discouraged by the prospect of a thesis written in Latin; in any case, the obscure *Quomodo Jacobi Amyot sermonem quidam d'Audiguier emendaverit* does not seem to have attracted much attention.

Although neither Le Breton nor Morillot saw fit to mention d'Audiguier in their histories of seventeenth-century French fiction, published in 1890 and 1892 respectively, the German literary

---

[93] ARDENNE DE TIZAC, dedicatory page.
[94] *Ibid.*, p. 42 f.
[95] *Ibid.*, p. 124.

historian Körting proved to be more catholic in the scope of his *Geschichte des französischen Romans im 17. Jahrhundert*, first published in 1885-87. D'Audiguier is mentioned but with little remaining lustre to his reputation; Körting speaks of him as the possible revisor of Amyot's Heliodorus and as the author of the "heute ganz verschollen" novels, *Lysandre et Caliste* and *Aristandre et Cléonice*.[96] Körting incorrectly attributes a 1618 translation of Cervantes' *Galatea* to him, probably confusing this work with *Persiles y Segismunda*.[97] As an added blow to a well-bruised posthumous reputation, Körting refers to him as Henri Vital d'Audiguier, confusing him with an unrelated lawyer of the following generation, even though this persistent confusion had been clarified as early as 1748 by Joly.[98]

Early in the twentieth century, two other German scholars took a more substantial interest in him. In an article published in 1909 on the origins of the psychological novel in France,[99] Walther Küchler declares d'Audiguier to be a significant precursor in this field as the author of *Les Diverses Affections*. According to Küchler, this is one of a number of hitherto forgotten novels of the early seventeenth century which along with Mareschal's better-known *Chrysolite* depart from fashionable idealism in their characterization and portrayal of contemporary life, yet which lack the deliberately satirical qualities of the *roman comique* or *satirique* in depicting social classes or professions. Küchler calls these the first "realistic-psychological novels of character" to be produced in France.[100] In his *Geschichte des französischen Romans* (1912), von Wurzbach reproduces both of Körting's mistakes in regard to d'Audiguier's name and his alleged translation of the *Galatea*;[101]

---

[96] HEINRICH KÖRTING, *Geschichte des französischen Romans im 17. Jahrhundert* (Zweite Ausgabe; Oppeln und Leipzig: Franck, 1891), p. 383 n.
[97] *Ibid.*, p. 65.
[98] *Ibid.*, p. 383. See Joly, p. 156 n.
[99] WALTHER KÜCHLER, "Zu den Anfängen des psychologischen Romans in Frankreich", *Archiv für das Studium der neureren Sprachen und Literaturen*, CXXIII (1909), 88-118.
[100] This idea is belittled in GUSTAVE REYNIER, *Le Roman réaliste au XVIIe siècle* (Paris: Hachette, 1914), p. 240.
[101] WOLFGANG VON WURZBACH, *Geschichte des französischen Romans: I. Band-Von den Anfängen bis zum Ende des XVII. Jahrhunderts* (Heidelberg: Carl Winter's Universitätsbuchhandlung, 1912), pp. 247 and 211.

having copied Körting, he then condenses the substance of Küchler's article, linking d'Audiguier's *Diverses Affections* and Du Verdier's *Larmes de Floride* with Mareschal's novel as slightly earlier and somewhat inferior manifestations of the same character analysis of a spirited coquette.[102] Von Wurzbach's presentation differs from Küchler's in its drastically simplified view of the psychological analysis undertaken in these novels.

Another instance of foreign scholarly interest in d'Audiguier at this time is seen in the article of an Italian critic, appearing in the University of Bordeaux *Bulletin italien* in 1906. Procacci's "Un romanzo francese del seicento e una sua traduzione italiana" is the most detailed discussion of *Lysandre et Caliste* since *Le Berger extravagant*.[103] Procacci also gives an analysis of the changes found necessary by its Italian translator in 1663.

Meanwhile in France d'Audiguier achieved a certain recognition in Reynier's *Le Roman sentimental en France avant l'Astrée* (1908). In a list of novelists of the period who wrote for profit appears his name with the comment,

> si glorieux de sa noblesse, qui composera longtemps aprés 1610 des histoires et des vers, mais dont le meilleur roman sera celui de sa vie aventureuse et tragique.[104]

Although the period covered by the book ends in 1610, Reynier makes extensive use of *La Flavie* and *Lydamant et Callyante* in his analysis of the fiction of the day, even though neither is technically a sentimental novel.

In Lachèvre's *Les Recueils collectifs de poésies libres et satiriques publiés depuis 1600 jusqu'à la mort de Théophile (1626)*, published in 1914, there is not only a good biographical sketch of d'Audiguier but also one of the fullest and most careful bibliographies ever done of his published works.[105] More recently, his

---

[102] *Ibid.*, pp. 351 ff.

[103] G. PROCACCI, "Un romanzo francese del seicento e una sua traduzione italiana", *Bulletin italien*, VI (1906), 219-33.

[104] REYNIER, *Le Roman sentimental*, p. 265. "Ce ne sont d'ailleurs pas ceux qui ont le plus de talent, mais comme ils ont accumulé les volumes, ils sont les seuls dont les noms soient passés, je ne dis pas à la postérité, mais du moins à la génération suivante" (*ibid.*).

[105] See LACHÈVRE, *Les Recueils collectifs*, pp. 157-61.

novels were exploited to advantage by Magendie in *Le Roman français au XVIIe siècle, de l'Astrée au Grand Cyrus* (1932); admittedly, the least happy features of d'Audiguier's technique and style seem to have been ferreted out and carefully noted. He fares somewhat better in Hainsworth's study of the publishing history of the *Novelas exemplares* in France (1933); while carrying no brief for any artistic excellence on the part of d'Audiguier, Hainsworth recognizes him as a writer of considerably greater influence than had been credited him in the past. Modestly (or politely) acknowledging that d'Audiguier's works had been "dépouillés d'une manière satisfaisante" by Ardenne de Tizac,[106] Hainsworth offers a five-page biographical and critical sketch better written and more useful than his predecessor's entire essay.[107] His discussion of d'Audiguier's role as a translator is careful and thorough; and his special bibliography of d'Audiguier's works ranks with Lachèvre's, with much added information.

No survey of a seventeenth-century French writer's present reputation would be complete without consulting the most important recent history of the literature of that period. Apart from scattered references to d'Audiguier's association with Marguerite's circle, Antoine Adam sums up his life and career in a laconic nine-line footnote.[108] He cites only the 1604 and 1614 poetry collections and mentions "plusieurs romans, notamment en 1606 et 1607".[109] No reference is made to d'Audiguier's work as a translator, and no indication is given of the title of his most significant novel, *Lysandre et Caliste*, in Adam's later mention of it in connection with the Du Ryer play based upon it.[110]

This apparent indifference on Adam's part is typical of the sort of difficulty continually besetting d'Audiguier's critical reputation during the past three hundred years. In each century, there has been at least one authoritative voice to present as thorough and as fair a picture of d'Audiguier's career as available informa-

---

[106] HAINSWORTH, *Les "Novelas exemplares"*, p. 45.
[107] *Ibid.*, pp. 45-50.
[108] ADAM, I, 104 n.
[109] *Ibid.*, p. 105 n.
[110] *Ibid.*, p. 484.

tion permitted, notably Colletet, Aubert, Barbier, and Hainsworth. These have been copied or reworked, usually in an abridged form which emphasizes only special aspects. And finally there have been critics and literary historians of equal or greater eminence who have disregarded the available information in their rapid and often inaccurate summaries of the life and career of a writer who deserved better of them.

Chapter III

TRADITIONAL MOTIFS, DEVICES, AND TECHNIQUES

In composing his novels, d'Audiguier was usually a thoroughgoing conformist who did not hesitate to exploit venerable, even threadbare literary conventions to his own advantage. Finding himself uncomfortably dependent on the sale of his writings for subsistence, he would naturally be attracted to material which had proved to be popular and saleable rather than to experimentation.

D'Audiguier's first novel, *La Flavie* (1606), followed a contemporary tendency to regard the novel as a sort of inferior epic written in prose,[1] combining love, war, and adventure in episodic form. Freely adapting and incorporating themes, characters, and episodes from well-known Latin, French, and Italian epic poetry, he portrays an immediately post-Trojan Gaul ruled by the lineal ancestors of the House of Bourbon, one of whom (Francus) is Hector's son, while Flavie herself is Hercules' granddaughter. In addition to the loves and adventures of the protagonists, there is an element of national destiny in the overcoming of precocious Spanish perfidy and evil by the irresistible justice and might of the first French king.

La Flavie contains also a pastoral episode of the traditional Arcadian sort. Although the innate nobility of Hector's and Penthesileia's adolescent son Pallante causes the youth to resent the frugality and isolation of the shepherds among whom he

---

[1] See MAGENDIE, *Le Roman français au XVIIe siècle*, pp. 125 ff.

has been reared, Prince Belysare is greatly attracted by their calm and wholesome existence. He is charmed by the bleating of

> les voix innocentes des tendres aigneaux, qui se marians aux agrestes sons d'une musette pastorale, faisoient alaigrement retentir les Echos des prochains vallons. [2]

The graceful dancing of the shepherdesses strikes him as a far better pastime than "les curieuses recerches de nos inventions, fonduës en la diversité de mille mols et delicieux plaisirs". [3] Even the pastoral diet of "de gras moutons", "de bons pastés de sanglier", and "de simples chastaignes virolées à la Lymosine" appeals to his princely appetite. [4] Pallante himself later expresses regret at abandoning this idyllic scene, where even the sheep on occasion are addressed with elegant verse.

Although both epic and pastoral motifs were permanently dropped by d'Audiguier after *La Flavie*, the influence of the sixteenth-century novel of chivalry persisted in each novel he wrote. No matter what the period of history, his principal male characters are invariably identified as *chevaliers*, with the expressed or implied corollary that each is also valorous and handsome. In *Lysandre et Caliste*, Henri IV is quickly persuaded to determine Lysandre's innocence or guilt by means of a full-blown trial by combat—"suivant les anciennes coustumes de ce Royaume" [5]— to be held in chivalric pomp on the site of the future Place Royale in Paris. *La Flavie's* neo-mythological Francus is obliged to overcome a monster in the best medieval tradition. Not only Ancient Gaul but seventeenth-century Paris and London resound to the clash of weapons in great invitation tournaments—irresistible to protagonists like Francus and Lysandre— under the patronage of the Kings, Queens, and Courts of France and England, a willful anachronism on d'Audiguier's part. Attempting to learn Lydamant's whereabouts, Palémon decides to camp near a strategic bridge and challenge every passing French knight either to win the right of passage in combat or to leave his name and that of

---

[2] AUDIGUIER, *La Flavie*, p. 6.
[3] *Ibid.*, p. 16.
[4] *Ibid.*, p. 17.
[5] AUDIGUIER, *Lysandre et Caliste*, p. 430.

his beloved to be displayed there on a sign. In this way, Palémon amasses some thousand names before Lydamant happens by, even though this takes places ostensibly within Henri IV's reign. Epic combats of great violence and often amazing duration occur frequently; even Adraste in *Les Diverses Affections* must battle with extraordinary vigor to overcome the thugs who twice waylay him at night in the streets of Paris.

The conventional chivalric code of personal honor is an important motivating factor in the reactions of major characters. It stirs maidens like Flavie and Callyante — as well as matrons like Caliste and Minerve — to single-minded zeal in preserving their reputations, and it obliges Francus, Filamor, Lydamant, Lysandre, and Aristandre to assert their valor in duels — or at least in seeking duels, like Adraste. It is noteworthy that the duel between Lysandre and Cloridan "en chemise", supposedly in Henri IV's reign, corresponds to d'Audiguier's own factual account of a duel which occurred nearly half a century before,[6] an anachronistic detail that suggests the literary conventionality of the motif.

Equally standard in the novel of chivalry is the often disquieting sensuality of its heroes and the relative complaisance of their ladies.[7] The result in d'Audiguier's novels is a consistent frankness in regard to sexual desire and its gratification. Flavie's near-seduction by the Prince of Spain is described in unambiguous language, as are the vigorous attempts which Lysandre makes on Caliste's virtue. Both Lydamant and Adraste are represented as being allowed bedroom caresses of perilous intimacy, although a similar situation does actually result in Silésie's disgrace during the Queen Marthésie episode of *Aristandre et Cléonice*. The sexual sophistication of both Lydamant and his disguised sister Statyre is such that neither is long confounded by the baldly direct proposition of the *châtelain*'s incontinent daughters; although Statyre cannot accept this offer, Lydamant proceeds to take full advantage of the situation with his benefactress, "et vange sur elle une partie

---

[6] See VITAL D'AUDIGUIER, *Le Vray et ancien usage des duels. Confirmé par l'exemple des plus illustres combats et deffys qui se soient faits en la Chrestienté* (Paris: C. Billaine, 1617), "Avertissement".

[7] See REYNIER, *Le Roman sentimental*, pp. 199 ff.

des cruautez de Callyante". [8] Statyre's would-be mistress voices her disappointment in memorable though unlikely terms:

> Quoy, dit-elle, vous payez donc mes affections d'un reffus? Vous méprisez donc ce que tant d'autres achetteroient au pris de leurs vies? ô l'ingratitude! ha! que les Cieux ont mal employé céte beauté qu'ilz ont mise sur ton visage. Va cruël, tu n'as point d'humanité dans le cœur, ny de cœur méme, si ce n'ét peut-étre de quelque Tygre. Va traître, vente-toy d'avoir méprisé les premiers fleurons de mon pucelage, la joye que tu en recevras en sera si courte que tu n'auras pas le loisir de la ressentir. [9]

D'Audiguier is equally candid in his references to the consummation of marriage. After the wedding banquet of Lydamant and Callyante, "Dieu! que de delices". [10] Following the multiple wedding and the festive jousts in its honor at the close of *Lysandre et Caliste*,

> il y eust bien un autre combat entre les cinq Mariez et leurs espousées, qui leur fut encore plus agreable. O Hymenée! que de merveilles, et que de gloire apres tant d'annuys! [11]

In an interpolated story in *Aristandre et Cléonice*, Polinice, finally released from an unintentional betrothal to a statue of Venus, kisses his faithful horse with delight as he prepares to return to consummate his marriage at last:

> Mais ce furent bien d'autres baisers, et d'autres embrassemens le soir mesme avec son Helise, recompensant tant de frayeurs par les delices d'une joüissance paisible. [12]

The sequence of events at the wedding of Tiribase and Orithie at the end of the same novel is bluntly presented:

---

[8] AUDIGUIER, *Lydamant et Callyante*, p. 79 A.
[9] *Ibid.*, p. 80 Bf.
[10] *Ibid.*, p. 144 A.
[11] AUDIGUIER, *Lysandre et Caliste*, p. 695.
[12] AUDIGUIER, *Aristandre et Cléonice*, p. 153.

Ils entrerent au Temple qu'il estoit desja bien tard, au sortir du Temple dans le festin, du festin au bal, et du bal au lit. [13]

The introduction of Arthurian lore in *Lysandre et Caliste* results in an incongruous situation at the great tournament given by James I. Not only do lineal descendants of knights of the Round Table compete as the English champions, but the chief prize —presented by the Prince of Wales— is a sword once owned by King Arthur himself. Such an anomaly is possibly intended to produce a mildly comic effect.

Although the bridge defender Palémon in *Lydamant et Callyante* is referred to only as a Black Knight, several of the sets of armor described in *Lysandre et Caliste* have heraldic devices and mottoes appropriate to the personality or situation of their owners — a conventional element in chivalric fiction. Convinced that Lysandre has cast her off in favor of Ypolite, the disconsolate Caliste prepares to die disguised as his champion in the forthcoming trial by combat; her armor for this occasion is black and bears a waterwheel device inscribed "los llenos de dolor y los vazios de sperança". [14] Meanwhile, preparing for the London tournament, Lysandre orders ashen-colored armor flecked with sparks and sown with lilies; its device is Love being burned at the stake by a lady, with the motto "Siempre constante". [15] Even more bizarre is the armor ordered by Lydian for the same tournament: Love is represented with a dart in his mouth and an olive branch in his hand on a blue background with gold stars; at Love's feet appears a goose with a stone in its bill; the motto is "Lëale et secreto". [16] Lysandre's implacable prosecutor Varasque appears before Henri IV in armor bearing the device of an ostrich holding a horseshoe in its beak, with the motto "Sic nutriuntur

---

[13] *Ibid.*, p. 382.
[14] Audiguier, *Lysandre et Caliste*, p. 455.
[15] *Ibid.*, p. 457. Lysandre later acquires a new and equally bizarre suit of armor: "Il fit relever un Aigle d'argent, ayant les aisles estendues et demy bruslees sous un Soleil d'or qu'il regardoit fixement, avecque ceste devise, *purche goden gli occhi, ardan le piume*" (*ibid.*, p. 570).
[16] *Ibid.*, p. 458.

fortes".[17] Near the end of the novel, Lysandre appears incognito at the Queen's contest in still another suit of armor: azure with gold stars forming the telltale constellation of the Great Bear (Callisto in mythology); his device is a dead lover mourned by a lady, with the motto "Sero probatur amor, qui morte probatur".[18] An instance of open heraldic parody occurs in *Les Diverses Affections*; Minerve and her rival Cariclée refer ironically to Adraste as their "Chevalier au cœur my-parti".[19]

Another area of fictional exploitation for d'Audiguier was the supernatural, evident in a variety of manifestations. Magic and magicians figure outright in three of the novels. In *La Flavie*, the evil designs of the Prince of Spain on Flavie's virtue are furthered by the magic of his devoted African knight Merlan, who is particularly skilled in causing weather phenomena: "... il faisoit la nuict claire, et le jour obscur, arrestoit le Soleil, et faisoit cheminer la terre".[20] Lysandre's seemingly mortal wounds from his ambush are promptly healed by an "opérateur" sought out by Lydian; this practitioner merely asks that Lysandre's torn and bloody doublet be brought to him for this to be accomplished. There are unpleasant after-effects, however, for Lysandre later falls gravely ill and astounds his Capuchin visitors by vomiting—among other things—"des ganifs, des escritoires, des images de Cire, des bracellets de cheveux, et des clous de charrette",[21] objects thereafter preserved as relics in the local monastery. This incident, explained by one of the monks, is attributed to a charm probably resulting from Lysandre's earlier supernatural cure,

> car le diable ne fait rien pour rien, et ne vous secourut en ceste extremité, que pour vous reduire en une plus grande.[22]

---

[17] *Ibid.*, p. 615 f.
[18] *Ibid.*, p. 669.
[19] AUDIGUIER, *Les Diverses Affections*, p. 72 A.
[20] AUDIGUIER, *La Flavie*, p. 53.
[21] AUDIGUIER, *Lysandre et Caliste*, p. 179.
[22] *Ibid.*, p. 185. The *opérateur*'s treatment *in absentia* anticipates Sir Kenelm Digby's description in 1658 of the "powder of sympathy" cure, requiring only that a bandage taken from a wound be placed in this powder.

During the wedding banquet at the close of *Lysandre et Caliste*, a nymph suddenly appears and dashes a vase to the floor, causing a terrifying storm within the hall; when the cloud disappears, the nymph has been replaced by a black marble obelisk bearing prophetic inscriptions in Spanish, Italian, and Old French. In the "Marriage to a Statue" story included in *Aristandre et Cléonice*, the hapless Polinice finally has recourse to the old magician Palombe, who was responsible for the troublesome magic ring which automatically makes any recipient the donor's bride — even statues, unfortunately. Palombe is able to undo the mischief but not without irritating his unearthly cohorts. In the same novel, the preaching monk Hiparque possesses magical skill which enables him to cast a spell over his victims' household, causing everyone except the object of his lust to fall into a deep slumber. When the police later search his monastery cell, they discover a lighted resin lamp; when this is extinguished, the household abruptly awakens.

Somewhat akin to magicians are astrologers and other seers, who also have their place in these novels. Flavie is guided through a sort of museum of future history by a white-clad, venerable old man, whose association with "les destins" enables him to inform her of the glorious future lying in store for her regal descendents in France. Regnier, the foster-father of Lydamant's sister Statyre, is not only a Venetian senator and former governor of Cyprus but also an accomplished cloud-watcher and astrologer who "predisoit l'advenir avec une certitude infaillible".[23] Since nothing escapes his observation, he is aware of Statyre's innocent passion for her unknown brother and of Lydamant's discouragement in his suit for Callyante; Regnier takes it upon himself to arrange a meeting of brother and sister and to assure Lydamant of the inevitability of his marriage to Callyante.

In *Lysandre et Caliste*, a mathematician named La Brosse manipulates figures and arrives at the conclusion that only a dead man will win the Queen's contest. This scornfully received prediction ultimately proves to be true when the contest is won by the Knight of the Dead Lover, Lysandre.

---

[23] AUDIGUIER, *Lydamant et Callyante*, p. 19 Bf.

In the final interpolated story of *Aristandre et Cléonice*, the penurious nobleman Tiribase, having decided to seek his fortune as a pirate who attacks only other pirates, seeks the counsel of an Arab seer before setting out. After attempting to dissuade him, the Arab finally offers an elaborate multiple prediction for him which enigmatically foresees violent reversals of fortune but an ultimately happy issue out of his afflictions. The story itself is told by Théodore —"mage de Perse" [24]— as an example of the sort of exact clairvoyance possible in predictions such as the one that has just been made by his physiognomist companion in regard to Cléonice's future husband.

Ghosts figure significantly in two of the novels. The ingenuous Flavie is understandably alarmed at the frightful apparition of her murdered escort, Prince Perses, who warns her of the lecherous intentions of her abductor. In *Lysandre et Caliste*, the ghost of a murdered Italian innkeeper, gratified by Cléandre's cooperation in finding and burying his body, agrees to warn him three days in advance of his death. The promise is all too soon made good by the grateful ghost after Cléandre's return to France, and three days after its warning Cléandre is murdered in his own home.

That venerable fictional device, the revelatory dream, proves useful in one important episode. The very night that Lysandre stealthily enters Beauplan for a secret rendezvous with Caliste, the latter's husband Cléandre is terrified by a dream in which Caliste is being abducted by a dragon; his coming to report this to her interrupts an already awkward interview and forces Lysandre to hide as best he can.

The fabulous voyage motif appears twice in these novels. Having sought the kidnaped Flavie throughout Europe and Africa, Francus finally boards a ship and is carried into the South Atlantic until the island of Virginie is sighted. After the pilot tells him its remarkable history, Francus disembarks and rides into a forest, where he is promptly attacked by a monster. Hastening back from Italy to France, Lydamant and Palémon are blown off course in the Mediterranean and are cast up near the Isle Volante

---

[24] AUDIGUIER, *Aristandre et Cléonice*, p. 308.

("Isle of Thieves"), a sort of anti-Utopia representing the worst features of modern French society. More conventional shipwrecks as well as pirate attacks befall voyagers in *Lysandre et Caliste* and *Aristandre et Cléonice.*

Among d'Audiguier's favorite traditional devices is the use of coincidence, standard in fiction and drama until a very recent date. The site chosen by Flavie's abductor for her undoing happens to be the very spot where Francus is camping for the night. Lydamant and Statyre happen to stop at the same inn and are thus able to meet for the first time. The traveler rescued from highwaymen by Lysandre happens to be Caliste's father, whose gratitude is not without effect on her complaisance toward Lysandre. Of all the Capuchin monks summoned to Lysandre's bedside, it is his old friend Clairange who happens to be called upon to exhort him to a Christian death. Cléandre, Lydian, and Lysandre all meet accidentally and under remarkable circumstances at Montserrat in Spain. Lysandre, Lydian, Alcidon, and Béronte all decide independently to participate in James I's tournament and are amazed to find themselves competing with one another in London. The murderer León happens to be lamenting his crime on the Jersey shore at the place where the falsely accused Lysandre is cast up by a Channel storm. Lysandre and Ypolite meet by chance on the road to Paris and engage in a violent duel. While the greater realism and reduced emphasis on adventure in *Les Diverses Affections* render coincidence unnecessary or at least inconspicuous in that novel, the vigorous career of the gentleman-pirate Tiribase in *Aristandre et Cléonice* is brought to a close with two improbable events. Having cast himself into a well as he is about to be jailed for fraud, Tiribase is rescued and found to be clutching a priceless jewelled collar which a runaway slave had stolen from his family years before and tossed into the well; even though this discovery is enough to restore his fortune, his economic recovery is reinforced by the unexpected arrival of his treasure-laden ships, which had been presumed lost at sea.

As might be expected, d'Audiguier makes considerable use of disguise and delayed recognition. His knights can easily conceal their identity with unfamiliar armor and closed visors, a situation which is especially common in *Lysandre et Caliste*. Lydamant's sister Statyre masquerades so successfully as a knight that not even her brother is aware of her true sex until the end of their trip, despite the enforced intimacy of traveling together. Both Caliste and Ypolite disguise themselves as knights in their determination to champion Lysandre's cause, a situation further complicated by Ypolite's appearance in Caliste's armor when encountered by Lysandre outside Paris. Within forty days, Lysandre has occasion to meet and ultimately to recognize Clairange in monk's garb, Cléandre in Algerian slave dress, and Lydian in the habit of a preaching hermit.

Like other novelists of the day, d'Audiguier occasionally advances the claim that he is offering a factual account rather than imaginary happenings. He claims to have heard Lysandre himself tell of his first seduction attempt on Caliste. The authenticity of the events in *Les Diverses Affections* is emphatically established at the outset, when d'Audiguier declares his unwillingness to write anything but the truth:

> la fable n'a point de part en ce discours, et l'Oursse que je me propose d'y suivre, est la Verité. [25]

However, it is sometimes possible for him to find a chink in the armor of verisimilitude to justify unlikely episodes, as in the following passage from *Lydamant et Callyante*:

> Plusieurs avantures leur arriverent en chemin, qui sont incroyables, et que j'aime mieux passer sous silence que revoquer en doute la verité de ceste histoire, par la nouveauté d'un discours qui pourroit sembler estrange, à ceux principalement qui ne sont pas accoustumez à telles fortunes. Mais parce qu'ils furent jettez en une isle qui n'avoit point encore esté descouverte, je suis content d'en dire les raretez... [26]

The conventional narrative techniques used by d'Audiguier constitute the most tiresome aspect of his novels, particularly in a lengthy one like *Lysandre et Caliste* where their continual repetition is all the more conspicuous. The overheard soliloquy en-

---

[25] AUDIGUIER, *Les Diverses Affections*, p. 3 B.
[26] AUDIGUIER, *Lydamant et Callyante*, p. 113 Bf.

ables him to reveal the sorcerer Merlan's whereabouts and condition to Marthésie in *La Flavie*, to identify Palémon to Lydamant, and to expose the essence of Lysandre's illicit passion to Caliste and her brother-in-law Béronte.[27]

His infrequent descriptions tend to be stylized and conventional, although in *Les Diverses Affections* his psychological realism results in a more original and interesting sort of commentary. His landscapes are limited to such generalities as "une plaine verdoyante de plusieurs prairies",[28] or "une belle campagne, arrosée des claires ondes de ce beau fleuve".[29] There is, for example, remarkably little difference between his description of the hilltop site of Callyante's country house in France and that of Senator Regnier's Venetian palace.

Like other novelists of the period, d'Audiguier often resorts to an elusive technique somewhat akin to the Ciceronian *praeteritio* whenever he is too hurried or too unsure of himself to undertake the description of a person, scene, or situation he wishes to mention.[30] On occasion, he inserts himself in his fiction as an omniscient author who comments on the action, apostrophizes the characters, or informs the reader of forthcoming reversals. This characteristic is comically evident at the end of *Lydamant et Callyante* and *Lysandre et Caliste* when, commenting on the wedding-night

---

[27] The use of the overheard soliloquy in novels is condemned by Charles Sorel in *De la connoissance des bons livres, ou examen de plusieurs autheurs* (Paris: A. Pralard, 1671), p. 120 f.

[28] AUDIGUIER, *La Flavie*, p. 6.

[29] AUDIGUIER, *Lysandre et Caliste*, p. 645.

[30] "De vous sçavoir dire ce qu'elle fit, ce qu'elle devint, combien de passions la frapperent toùt à la fois, il n'est pas possible seulement de l'imaginer" (*Lydamant et Callyante*, p. 131 B); "Ils dirent plusieurs autres choses qui seroient longues à raconter..." (*Lysandre et Caliste*, p. 297); "Plusieurs autres discours se passerent entr'eux qui pourroient embellir ceste histoire, si nous n'aymions mieux raconter les choses que les parolles" (*ibid.*, p. 125); "...et apres succederent des Adieux si pitoyables, que je n'en veux point affliger davantage les lecteurs de ceste histoire, car la tristesse est si contagieuse..." (*ibid.*, p. 347); "Je renvoye à l'histoire ceux qui voudront voir les autres particularitez de la prise de ceste place..." (*Les Diverses Affections*, p. 81 A). This device is condemned by Sorel as evidence of incompetence (*De la connoissance des bons livres*, p. 125).

bliss of the protagonists, d'Audiguier expresses the hope that he too may enjoy such well-earned transports.

By using the ancient *histoire enclavée* technique of stories fitted within other stories like a set of concentric Chinese ivory balls, d'Audiguier produces a chain of narration in *La Flavie*. The dying Filamor's story is overheard by a soldier who later repeats it verbatim to Prince Belysare, Pallante, and the shepherds.

Another conventional technique frequently used by d'Audiguier is the casting of dialogue in lengthy speeches introduced solely by the name (often abbreviated) of the character speaking. Such an awkward method appears to be the result of a strong influence of the drama at this early moment in the development of the modern novel.

Equally irritating to modern fictional taste is d'Audiguier's technique of attempting to maintain simultaneous episodes, shifting abruptly from one to another in an effort to further the illusion. In *La Flavie*, Francus is left on the point of meeting the unknown benefactor who has helped him slay the monster on the island of Virginie, for the author declares that it is time to return to the Amazon Marthésie, "qui me reprochant mon oubly, me commande de laisser icy ce discours".[31] Books IX and X of *Lysandre et Caliste* are filled with juxtaposed scenes occurring in Paris, London, Gascony, Normandy, Burgundy, Jersey, and the Ile-de-France countryside; the author moves from one to another in a manner intended to convey a sense of immediacy:

> Revenons maintenant à Caliste que nous avons laissée si longuement errer toute seule, et voyons ce qu'elle devint...[32] Nous l'avons laissé flottant entre Douvre et Calais avec ses trois compagnons d'armes...[33] Cependant...Lysandre...escoutoit cest homme inconnu que nous avons laissé se complaignant en ceste sorte...[34]

However, it should be recalled that his technique —in a more subtle form, to be sure— has had its distinguished advocates in our own century, including André Gide and Aldous Huxley.

---

[31] AUDIGUIER, *La Flavie*, p. 169.
[32] AUDIGUIER, *Lysandre et Caliste*, p. 453.
[33] *Ibid.*, p. 509.
[34] *Ibid.*, p. 565.

As to d'Audiguier's literary sources, a number of episodes and motifs in these novels can be traced to probable antecedents. Some are merely adaptations of tried-and-true themes of specific origin; others are surprisingly direct borrowings incorporated in his text with little modification.

This exploitation extends back into the fictional materials of Roman and Byzantine antiquity. In Book VI of the *Aeneid*, the Cumæan Sibyl conducts Aeneas to the underworld, where his old father Anchises reveals to him a spectacular array of the future rulers of Rome down to the time of Augustus. This is the original but not exclusive source for the analogous scene in *La Flavie*, in which Hercules' granddaughter Flavie is led through the earth into an antipodal vale by a guide equal to Anchises in venerability; there she is shown the future kings of France down to the time of Henri IV and Louis XIII. D'Audiguier is also apparently indebted to Virgil for his conclusion of *La Flavie*, an abruptly terminated scene in which the Amazon Marthésie, momentarily compassionate toward the evil magician-knight she has just defeated, wrathfully slays him upon recognizing his sword as having belonged to the murdered Prince Perses.[35]

Pliny the Younger is the likely source of d'Audiguier's "Grateful Ghost" episodes in Books IV and VI of *Lysander et Caliste*. Oddly enough, they constitute a fusion of two separate anecdotes recounted in the *Letters*; for Pliny first tells of a ghost which appeared to a traveler to predict his death, then of another ghost which persistently haunted a house until a courageous philosopher learned from it that the proper burial of its bones would lay it to rest.[36]

Heliodorus' *Ethiopian Romance* (*Theagenes and Chariclea*) was unusually familiar to d'Audiguier as the revisor of Amyot's popular translation of it. In *Lysandre et Caliste*, first published six years after this revision appeared, Cléandre dreams that a dragon

---

[35] Cf. *Aeneid*, XII, ll. 938-52. Having defeated Turnus in single combat, Aeneas is moved by pity for his now helpless rival and is on the point of sparing his life. Suddenly he notices that Turnus is wearing the studded belt of young Pallas, whom Turnus had slain. All pity vanishes as Aeneas wrathfully plunges his sword into Turnus' breast.

[36] See PLINY THE YOUNGER, *Letters*, VII, no. xxvii.

is abducting his wife the very night that Lysandre intends to seduce her; this bears more than a casual resemblance to Charicles' dream that an eagle is abducting his adopted daughter Chariclea while arrangements for her elopement are being completed.[37] The cave love-scene which makes Theagenes' continence so difficult[38] resembles those indulged in by the passionate Lysandre and by Adraste in *Les Diverses Affections*. More direct still is d'Audiguier's adaptation for *La Flavie* of the recognition scene in which Theagenes and Chariclea are saved *in extremis* from sacrifice by the arrival of old Charicles;[39] the Virginie episode narrated to Francus by his pilot is an only slightly modified version of this, including its final joyous abolition of human sacrifice.

Medieval literature provided further materials for these novels. The Indo-European fictional tradition (perhaps antedated in this respect by Egyptian and Oriental lore) has long had the narrative device of a vindictive woman who attempts to discredit and ruin a young nobleman by telling the King a series of pointed stories; and this is the basis of the structure of *Aristandre et Cléonice*. Just which earlier version d'Audiguier adapted is uncertain, but the Old French *Sept Sages de Rome* is probably as likely a source as any in view of its wide dissemination in France during the late Middle Ages and the Renaissance.[40] The "Marriage to a Statue" story in *Aristandre et Cléonice* is a celebrated medieval tale — "The Bachelor of Rome", with the magician Palumbus — of which the first known version appears in William of Malmesbury's *De Gestis Regum Anglorum* and which was spread through-

---

[37] See Heliodorus, *An Ethiopian Romance*, trans. Moses Hadas (Ann Arbor: University of Michigan Press, 1957), p. 100.

[38] *Ibid.* p. 113.

[39] *Ibid.*, pp. 248 ff.

[40] At least three editions of it were published in Geneva during the 1490's. Editions published in Lyon in 1577 and 1610 were available to d'Audiguier, as were perhaps two undated editions published in Paris and Lyon. See ROBERT BOSSUAT, *Manuel bibliographique de la littérature française du Moyen Age* (Melun: Librairie d'Argences, 1951), p. 132 f.; JACQUES-CHARLES BRUNET, *Manuel du libraire et de l'amateur de livres* (Paris: Firmin-Didot, 1860-65, V, cols. 295-97; *ibid.*, *Supplément par MM. P. Deschamps et G. Brunet* (Paris: Firmin-Didot, 1878-80), II, cols. 636-37; *British Museum Catalogue of Printed Books: 1881-1900* (Vol. 47; Ann Arbor: J. W. Edwards, 1946), col. 385.

out Western Europe by later chroniclers and collectors of tales.[41] D'Audiguier's version is apparently the first manifestation of the legend in modern French fiction.[42]

Several of the great Renaissance epics are reflected in these novels. The warrior maidens Marthésie (*La Flavie*) and Statyre (*Lydamant et Callyante*) both appear to be versions of Ariosto's lover-seeking Bradamante in *Orlando Furioso*; Ypolite (*Lysandre et Caliste*) seems to have been inspired in part by Tasso's self-made Amazon Clorinda in *Gerusalemme Liberata*, whose combats with her unsuspecting lover Tancredi are imitated in the duel between the disguised Ypolite and her beloved Lysandre.[43]

Although the *Aeneid* is the likely original source for Flavie's glimpse of her glorious posterity, two famous Renaissance adaptations of Virgil's episode probably contributed much to d'Audiguier's version. In Book IV of *Orlando Furioso*, Bradamante is taken into the grotto of Merlin's tomb, where she is shown her descendents of the House of Este. In Book IV of the later and considerably less successful *Franciade*, Ronsard describes Francus' visit to the underworld, guided by the pseudo-witch Hyante, who identifies for him the shades appearing in a misty whirlwind:

> par ce moyen [Francus] apprend sommairement l'un apres l'autre les noms des Rois de France, les actes infames des vicieux, et les gestes magnanimes des vertueux.[44]

Ronsard's Francus in turn was probably inspired by the neo-mythological figure of this name who appears in Jean Lemaire de Belges' *Illustrations de Gaule et singularités de Troie* (1511-13).[45]

---

[41] See PAULL FRANKLIN BAUM, "The Young Man Betrothed to a Statue", *PMLA*, XXIV (1919), 523-79.

[42] The likelihood of d'Audiguier's influence on Mérimée's "La Vénus d'Ille" is dismissed in MAGENDIE, *Le Roman français au XVIIe siècle*, p. 421.

[43] See TORQUATO TASSO, *La Gerusalemme Liberata* (Firenze: Felice Le Monnier, 1853), III, xxff. and XII, xlixff. The character of Clorinda is briefly analyzed in FREDI CHIAPPELLI, "Clorinda", *Studi Tassiani*, IV (1954), 19-22.

[44] PIERRE DE RONSARD, *La Franciade*, in *Oeuvres*, ed. Paul Laumonier (Paris: Lemerre, 1914-18), III, 8 ("Argument au quatrieme livre"). Unlike Ronsard, who breaks off his list at Pépin, d'Audiguier projects Flavie's revelation as far as Louis XIII, with no suggestion of any "vicieux" descendants capable of "actes infames".

[45] The genesis of the character Francus is discussed in GEORGES DOUTRE-

As a reluctant hispanist, d'Audiguier was familiar with a number of contemporary works of Spanish prose fiction and did not scruple to exploit some of them in his own. Hainsworth has already pointed out the derivation of Lysandre's rescue of Caliste's former jailer from an escort of archers; [46] this is apparently an imitation of Cervantes' episode in which Don Quixote disperses the guards escorting a group of galley-slaves, although Lysandre's indignation at the idea of human captivity is wholly feigned. [47] Likewise, d'Audiguier's description of the moral downfall of Caliste's attendant Clarinde and her subsequent exploitation of her mistress' compromised position has an antecedent in *Don Quixote*; the noble Camila finds herself in just such a situation with her increasingly brazen servant Leonela in the interpolated story of "El Curioso Impertinente". [48] Having just completed his translation of six of Cervantes' *Novelas exemplares* at the time *Lysandre et Caliste* was published, d'Audiguier seems to be indebted to one of them — "La Española Inglesa" — for Cléandre's tale of capture by an Algerian pirate off Genoa, although his subsequent rescue off Barcelona is a departure from Cevantes' plot. [49] Lope de Vega's *El Peregrino en su patria*, translated by d'Audiguier the preceding year, seems to have been the source of the Montserrat episode in that same novel; the simultaneous pilgrimages of Lysandre and Cléandre as well as Lydian's brief retirement there as a hermit were probably suggested by a Montserrat pilgrimage episode in Lope's novel. [50]

PONT, *Jean Lemaire de Belges et la Renaissance* (Bruxelles: Hayez, 1934), p. 61 f.

[46] See GEORGE HAINSWORTH, "Cervantes en France: à propos de quelques publications récentes", *Bulletin hispanique*, XXXIV (1932), 136 f.

[47] Cf. MIGUEL DE CERVANTES SAAVEDRA, *El Ingenioso Hidalgo Don Quixote de la Mancha*, ed. Rodríguez Marín (Madrid: Ediciones Atlas, 1947-49), II, ch. xxii.

[48] *Ibid.*, III, ch. xxxiv, especially p. 78 f.

[49] See MIGUEL DE CERVANTES SAAVEDRA, "La Española Inglesa", in *Novelas ejemplares* (Buenos Aires: Editorial Araujo, 1939), II, 229 f. Cf. Vital d'Audiguier, trans., "L'Espagnolle Angloise", in *Les Nouvelles de Michel Cervantes* (Paris: Jean Richer, 1621), II, 50 f.

[50] See LOPE, FELIX, DE VEGA CARPIO, *El Peregrino en su patria* (in *Colección de las obras sueltas, assi en prosa, como en verso*; Tomo V; Madrid: Antonio de Sancha, 1776), Libro II. But whereas Lope's original text portrays foreign pilgrims unanimous and expansive in their praise of Spain

Two other contemporary authors possibly imitated by d'Audiguier have been indicated by modern scholars. Although the character of Minerve in *Les Diverses Affections* is one of his most interesting and original efforts, her personality and basic situation may have their prototype in Honoré d'Urfé's *Astrée*; the attractive young widow in its interpolated "Histoire de Stelle" is a compulsive flirt who selfishly evades commitment to any suitor.[51] D'Audiguier's satirical description of an imaginary "Isle of Thieves" in Lydamant et Callyante, a bitter commentary on contemporary mores, closely resembles a similar description in the *Mundus alter et idem*, an unusual Rabelaisian work published anonymously around 1605 by Joseph Hall, Bishop of Exeter and Norwich.[52] In his vigorous neo-Latin assault on excesses and shortcomings of the age in this anti-Utopia, which became a European classic in the seventeenth century, Bishop Hall included a section on the Kingdom of Thieves (Lavernia) where a grasping materialism pervades all levels of society. If this is d'Audiguier's source, his prompt acquaintance with the work is noteworthy; for *Lydamant et Callyante* was published early in 1607.

It is clear that d'Audiguier was highly eclectic in his exploitation of literary antecedents. The scope of his probable borrowings is impressive, ranging from the first-century Virgil and Pliny to the seventeenth-century Anglican bishop Joseph Hall, d'Urfé, Cervantes, and Lope de Vega. The variety of traditional materials used and specific authors imitated suggests not only an energetic quest for the saleable but also a degree of literary erudition not anticipated in a man of d'Audiguier's unscholarly background.

---

and the Inquisition, d'Audiguier's translation eliminates all such passages (*Panfile et Nise*, Livre II). Furthermore, the *Lysandre et Caliste* episode is marked by a wholly unsympathetic attitude toward the Spanish. The name Ypolite (*Lysandre et Caliste*) may have been suggested by that of a converted Moorish girl in Lope's novel (*El Peregrino*, p. 333); see d'Audiguier, *Panfile et Nise*, p. 250.

[51] KÜCHLER, p. 95. See HONORÉ D'URFÉ, *L'Astrée*, Première Partie, ed. Hugues Vaganay (Lyon: Masson, 1925), pp. 181-94.

[52] HAINSWORTH, *Les "Novelas exemplares"*, p. 45 n. See JOSEPH HALL, *The Discovery of a New World (Mundus alter et idem)*, trans. John Healey, ed. Huntington Brown (Cambridge: Harvard University Press, 1937), pp. 124-36 (Book IV).

Chapter IV

REFLECTIONS OF CONTEMPORARY LIFE

Throughout d'Audiguier's novels appear elements of a topical nature, varying in diversity and frequency with each work. Although these are relatively oblique in *La Flavie*'s epic portrayal of Ancient Gaul and its noble Trojan refugees, references and allusions to conditions and attitudes of the early seventeenth century are introduced directly in each of his four other novels.

Among the most conspicuous of these elements is the life-long royalist d'Audiguier's praise for the French Crown, an adulation which is particularly fulsome in regard to the monarch reigning at the time each novel was published. As a particularly attractive figure to a Gascon gentleman-author, Henri IV is introduced spectacularly in *La Flavie* during the revelation to Princess Flavie of the whole line of French kings to be descended from Francus and herself. Although all impress her favorably,[1] she is particularly struck by one imposing figure; and her guide commends her well-placed curiosity:

> Il s'appellera HENRY LE GRAND, quatrieme du nom, Roy de France et de Navarre, tres-Chrestien, tres-Auguste, et tres-victorieux. Contre cestui-cy s'armeront toutes les nations de l'Europe pour le garder de monter au Throsne

---

[1] "...partout elle remarque quelque particuliere grace du Ciel, que Dieu doit faire pleuvoir sur ses successeurs. Bref, elle n'en void aucun qui ne soit avantageusement parti de quelques marques et qualités non seulement au dessus du commun des hommes, mais aussi des Princes." (AUDIGUIER, *La Flavie*, p. 142.)

de ses majeurs. Mais autant d'oppositions, autant de marches pour y parvenir; elles ne seront sitost formées, que vuidées. ²

After examining a scroll listing the perilous and glorious events of Henri IV's career, Flavie inquires as to the identity of the princess shown disarming him that he may be "aussi gracieux et doux en amour, comme il est terrible et insupportable en ses armes": ³

> Ha! dit le sage vieillard, que vous touchés bien maintenant la plus délicate piece de cest ouvrage; Sachez, ma fille, que ce grand Roy aprés avoir reüny ses sujets divisés, vangé l'honneur de la France, outragée par les estrangers, et effroyé de sa reputation les plus esloignés Potentats du monde; viendra rendre les palmes et les lauriers de ses triomphes entre les mains de ceste beauté, mille fois heureuse, et encore mille fois de voir tant de glories captives dessoubs ses pieds. ⁴

After further enthusiastic remarks, Flavie's guide reveals this remarkable woman to be Marie de Médicis, "qui doit ramener l'age d'or en France et replanter les Oliviers pres des Lys". ⁵ An equally glorious career is predicted for Marie's son, the future Louis XIII,

> dont la fortune ne sera jamais bornee, à qui la mer et la terre feront hommage, et à qui les Cieux contribueront les influences de leurs plus benignes constellations. Ha! Prince que de choses sont encloses en tes destinees! que d'oracles ont predit de toy les Sybills: par toy sera l'Univers appellé la France, et tant de Royaumes qu'il y a separez au monde, compris en une seule Monarchie. ⁶

In *Lydamant et Callyante*, set in the reign of "le grand Henry", ⁷ d'Audiguier resorts to essentially the same device in order to demonstrate his royalist loyalty. While waiting for the Venetian senator-astrologer Regnier to welcome them to his palace, Lyda-

---

² *Ibid.*, p. 143 f.
³ *Ibid.*, p. 145.
⁴ *Ibid.*, p. 145 f.
⁵ *Ibid.*, p. 146 f.
⁶ *Ibid.*, p. 147.
⁷ Audiguier, *Lydamant et Callyante*, p. 36 A.

mant and his sister Statyre have an opportunity to examine a series of painted mythological figures displayed in the great hall. They particularly admire that of a Poliocertes, "ce grand astre qui de la lumiere de sa gloire efface l'honneur de tous les guerriers passez, et l'esperance de tous les presens". [8] Equally impressive is the figure of Poliocertes' enchantress, "céte Lamye, qui pour n'avoir rien au monde de semblable, ne peut étre comparee qu'à elle méme". [9] She is well proportioned in every respect, "hormis en sa beauté qui étoit extréme". [10] Near these two figures appears an infant prince —with the eyes of one and the heart of the other— who has at his feet a downfallen empire which is beseeching him to raise it up again:

> C'ét enfant se pleignoit des victoires de son pere, et les voyoit à regret; craignant qu'il vainquit tout, et ne luy laissat rien à conquerir quand il seroit grand. [11]

Although assassinated five years before the publication of *Lysandre et Caliste* in 1615, Henri IV figures prominently in its plot; it is largely his initial displeasure and later change of heart which bring about the flight, vindication, and marriage of the protagonists. As "le plus valeureux Prince du monde" [12] and "pere...de nostre invincible Monarque", [13] Henri is represented as a vigorous paternal ruler who is somehow able to assume direct jurisdiction over two rather sordid murder cases arising in the novel. Apart from his taste for tournaments and other violent sports, he is transformed in this novel from a witty but rough Gascon ex-soldier into an exceptionally gracious and eloquent courtier. When Ypolite is presented to him upon the suspension of her trial-by-combat defense of Lysandre before the assembled Court and interested parties, the King gallantly reverses protocol by kissing her hands and presents her to the Queen with spontaneously elegant compliments unlikely in the mouth of the real *Vert-Galant*. Hailed as "un parfait exemple de

---

[8] *Ibid.*, p. 89 Bf.
[9] *Ibid.*, p. 90 A.
[10] *Ibid.*
[11] *Ibid.*, p. 90 B.
[12] AUDIGUIER, *Lysandre et Caliste*, p. 624.
[13] *Ibid.*, p. 1.

toutes vertus", [14] Marie appears at his side during several tournaments and even awards a prize ring during the pre-nuptial festivities which occur near the end of the novel. The supernatural apparition of a prophetically incribed obelisk during the final wedding feast enables d'Audiguier not only to deplore Henri's death and Marie's Regency problems but also to hail Louis XIII's recent marriage to Anne d'Autriche. [15]

In addition to the French royal family, members of the English House of Stuart also figure in *Lysandre et Caliste*. Having won the great tournament in London, Lysandre accepts his prizes from the Prince of Wales and his sister Elizabeth, the future Princess Palatine; however, he patriotically declines the offer of a pension from their father James I. D'Audiguier's references to English royalty are entirely unpolemical.

Royalist adulation is understandably restrained in the realistic narration of *Les Diverses Affections*, usually appearing only implicitly in the enthusiasm shown by Adraste for accompanying Louis XIII on military campaigns. [16] However, a familiar note does resound in the summary of Louis' Normandy campaign of 1621:

> L'histoire de ce siege n'estant point de nostre subjet, nous nous contenterons de dire que le bon-heur, la prevoyance, le conseil, et la diligence du Roy, luy conquirent ceste place en moins de trois jours, et trois jours apres toute ceste grande Province. [17]

The pseudo-Persian setting of *Aristandre et Cléonice* permits d'Audiguier to return to his earlier and more florid praise. In

---

[14] *Ibid.*, p. 674.

[15] After commenting on the publishing success of this "œuvre copieuse", Bourgeois and André reject it as "inutilisable pour l'historien; à la fin seulement quelques rares allusions aux mariages espagnols. Royaliste convaincu: style ampoulé" (EMILE BOURGEOIS ET LOUIS ANDRÉ, *Les Sources de l'histoire de France: XVIIe siècle [1610-1715]*, IV: Journaux et pamphlets ["Manuels de bibliographie historique: Les Sources de l'histoire de France depuis les origines jusqu'en 1815", part III, vol. XIV] [Paris: August Picard, 1924], p. 110).

[16] Cf. FRANÇOIS-TRISTAN L'HERMITE, *Le Page disgracié* (ed. Auguste Dietrich; Paris: Plon, 1898), Seconde Partie, chs. xlix-liii, for a similar description of some of the same campaigns and attitudes.

[17] AUDIGUIER, *Les Diverses Affections*, p. 75 Af.

describing the "Persian court" at "Persepolis", he is free to hail Louis XIII in the guise of the young Sophy Lysidor:

> Monarque genereux sur tous les Monarques, qui a toutes les vertus et perfections des autres Roys, sans avoir un seul de leurs vices, ni de leurs defauts: et qui ne manque que d'un Alexandre aussi grand que luy, pour luy oster autant d'honneur et de gloire qu'il en acquit sur les Perses, et pour trouver au monde quelque ennemy qui fust digne de son courage, et de sa valeur. [18]

Anne d'Autriche, as the "Hiberian" Queen Albanie, is represented as Lysidor's gracious and sophisticated consort. The politically unreliable Marie de Médicis reappears as a character in the narration of an incident said to have occurred in the household of Queen Mother Marthésie, whose generosity is abused by those whom she befriends; "la courtoisie, et le courage heroïque et genereux au dela de la mesme generosité la rendoient moins recommandable qu'adorable". [19] It is perhaps significant that the father of a disgraced lady-in-waiting unwisely suggests to Marthésie that the example of her own court was probably responsible for the girl's downfall.

The figure of Richelieu is also judiciously represented in the character of Lysidor's trusted chief minister, the powerful but gracious Alcandre:

> Aussi n'eust-on sceu dire s'il avoit plus de preud'hommie ou plus de prudence, plus de jugement ou plus de courage. [20]

Contrary to envious slander which accuses him of taking advantage of Lysidor's youth and kindness in order to arrogate royal power to himself "pour la ruine de ses ennemis, et pour l'establissement de ses serviteurs", [21] Alcandre-Richelieu has accepted only a small part of the authority offered him by Lysidor-Louis — and even that with reluctance:

---

[18] AUDIGUIER, *Aristandre et Cléonice*, p. 3.
[19] *Ibid.*, p. 214.
[20] *Ibid.*, p. 13.
[21] *Ibid.*, p. 16.

les hommes et les charges que les Roys sont importunez de donner aux autres, il estoit importuné de luy de les recevoir. [22]

Equally topical is d'Audiguier's support of "raison d'Etat", a doctrine of the Richelieu ministry which claimed unquestioning obedience to its disposition of subjects' affairs. Having been ordered by the Sophy to marry another woman despite his initial vow to accept only Cléonice, Aristandre explains his prompt submission to the royal will:

> Il est vray, Cleonice, que les enfans peuvent estre forcez de leurs peres, mais les hommes le peuvent estre aussi de leurs Roys, mesmes aux choses plus libres: Et les lois de l'Estat ont tant d'avantage en cela par dessus les loix naturelles, que le pere dont le fils doit estre sujet par la loy de la nature, peut estre sujet du fils par celle de l'Estat. Et si cela n'estoit point, ils ne seroient point nos Souverains, ny nous ne serions point leurs sujets. [23]

Although initially suspicious of Aristandre's logic in this explanation, Cléonice finally concedes the propriety of his decision:

> Vivez, Aristandre, avecque Luciane, puis que le destin et la Majesté Royale le veulent ainsi. [24]

D'Audiguier has harsh words for those factions which offer resistance to Richelieu's attempt to consolidate political power in the Crown. In *Les Diverses Affections*, Minerve's second husband, the former Parisian magistrate Tatius, unwisely allows his ambition of becoming Garde des Sceaux to involve him in a conspiracy against the government. This seditious effort, quickly frustrated, is ironically described:

> quelques Princes s'armerent pour la reformation de l'Estat, et le soulagement du peuple, que les soldats soulagerent bravement en les deschargeant de tout ce qu'ils pouvoyent emporter. [25]

---

[22] *Ibid.*
[23] *Ibid.*, p. 303 f.
[24] *Ibid.*, p. 306.
[25] AUDIGUIER, *Les Diverses Affections*, p. 72 Af.

The author deplores the continual divisions in France which precipitated one terrible crisis after another, especially during the King's youth. No sooner is Tatius' scheme overwhelmed than Louis XIII must subdue rebellion in Normandy, then Huguenot insubordination in Béarn and at La Rochelle, seat of "ceste belle assemblée" which d'Audiguier vigorously condemns. [26]

The Huguenots get short shrift in these novels, for d'Audiguier had no use for Protestants doctrinally or politically. In *Lysandre et Caliste*, most heresies are attributed to the evil work of debauched and apostate monks (e.g. Luther), "qui comme vipereaux taschent de crever en naissant les flancs de leur mere". [27] This anti-Protestant bias also appears to be reflected in d'Audiguier's brief fictional account of his lackey Jean Hélias' miraculous conversion to Roman Catholicism.

Another current prejudice is apparent in d'Audiguier's anti-Spanish bias. Flavie barely escapes seduction by the Prince of Spain, who is an incarnation of the *leyenda negra* of Spanish pride, lust, and underhanded vindictiveness. However, neither he nor his supporters are any match for the peerless Francus, founder of the French Kingdom. The advent of a Spanish princess as Queen of France in 1614 is probably responsible in part for the greater restraint in the Hispanophobia of *Lysandre et Caliste*; yet there is no mistaking d'Audiguier's sentiments. [28] The pre-eminence of a silver lamp on the high altar at Montserrat despite the presence of a more costly gold one is unblushingly explained as the result of a supernatural phenomenon which invariably causes the former —a gift of the French King— to be moved to the most prominent position despite the efforts of the monks to keep the Spanish King's gold lamp displayed there. In the same episode, pilgrims are amazed at the brilliant clarity and directness of the young hermit's sermon, "bien qui parlast Espagnol". [29]

> Bref, il estoit si parfait: que nos Pelerins qui estoient nais et nourris en la pureté de nostre air François, trouverent

---

[26] *Ibid.*, p. 111 A.
[27] AUDIGUIER, *Lysandre et Caliste*, p. 188.
[28] AUDIGUIER, *Les Diverses Affections*, p. 77 B.
[29] AUDIGUIER, *Lysandre et Caliste*, p. 205.

estrange que l'Espagne eut pû produire un si bel esprit.
...il n'avoit rien d'Espagnol que la langue...[30]

Their amazement is well founded, for the hermit is in reality Caliste's brother Lydian, who has temporarily retired to the contemplative life. D'Audiguier's continued deference to Anne d'Autriche in his portrayal of Queen Albanie in *Aristandre et Cleónice* allows only one guarded instance of his bias; Albanie's "Hiberian" lady-in-waiting Marianne has a strong Hispanic tendency to vindictiveness:

> C'estoit l'instrument le plus propre qu'[Arsilée] eust pû choisir à sa vengeance, tant pour estre tres-puissante auprés de la Reyne, que pour estre d'un naturel non moins prompt à se ressentir d'une injure, que tardif à la pardonner.[31]

Specific references to actual districts, streets, and buildings establish the Parisian setting in two of the novels. It is gratifying to be able to trace much of the activity in *Lysandre et Caliste* on a contemporary Paris street plan, in particular the movements involved in Lysandre's establishment of a stake-out near the Petit Châtelet prison and Caliste's subsequent rescue from it.[32] D'Audiguier has Lysandre's post-Rimbergue tournament take place in the Arsenal square, explaining that the Place Royale (the future Place des Vosges) had not as yet been built. However, the horse-market site of the Place Royale is used later in the novel for the trial-by-combat episode as well as for the public display of Caliste's unidentified armor. The quintuple wedding at the close of the novel is splendidly solemnized in the Bourbon Chapel of the Louvre itself. Caliste's Longchamps convent and Lysandre's Mont Valérien hermitage have an air of topographical reality in the precision of d'Audiguier's references to them; the author even claims to have visited the Mont Valérien hermitages in the company of the King and Queen.

---

[30] *Ibid.*, p. 206 f.
[31] AUDIGUIER, *Aristandre et Cléonice*, p. 207 f.
[32] An illustration and description of this prison (razed in 1782) appear in PHILIP G. HAMERTON, *Paris in Old and Present Times* (London: Seeley, 1892), p. 82.

The same type of realism is used in *Les Diverses Affections*. Like Olinde and Lydian in *Lysandre et Caliste*, Minerve and Adraste take walks together in the Tuileries gardens; but they also stroll through the Luxembourg and Saint-Germain gardens as well as the more distant ones at Rueil. It is while returning from Rueil that their carriage nearly topples into the Seine from the new Pont de Neuilly. [33]

More interesting still are the routes used by Adraste to reach Minerve's house, for here d'Audiguier outdoes himself with specific details. Early in the novel, Adraste and others are attacked by robbers just outside the city near Saint-Germain des Prés, "à l'endroit du puits qui est dedans la ruë à quelques cinquante pas de l'Abbaye". [34] Dispersing these assailants, Adraste pursues one of them until the robber is "aculé contre la barriere des Sergens qui est au bout de la mesme ruë". [35] Soon after, in a moment of panic, Adraste charges into an approaching group of strangers, who are later discovered to be a company of actors on their way into the city to play before Monsieur le Prince, accompanied along the way by a number of magistrates and their wives. Near the end of the novel, Adraste is again attacked while going from his lodgings near the Seine to Minerve's in the recently developed area near the Foire Saint-Germain; as he proceeds along the road which borders the moat between the Porte de Nesle and the Porte de Buci (the present Rue Mazarine), he is set upon by ruffians who at first pretend to be seeking the way to the nearby Porte Saint-Germain. [36] Both incidents reflect the great danger to which Parisians were subjected by gangs of thieves if they ventured into the streets at

---

[33] This crossing seems to have been notoriously dangerous in the seventeenth century. Prior to the construction of a wooden bridge around 1620, the crossing was accomplished by means of a ferry, on which Henri IV and the Queen were nearly drowned in 1606, according to Marquis de Rochegude et Maurice Dumolin, *Guide pratique à travers le vieux Paris* (Paris: Librairie ancienne Edouard Champion, 1923), p. 355. A similar carriage accident on this bridge befell Pascal in 1654.

[34] AUDIGUIER, *Les Diverses Affections*, p. 9 B.

[35] *Ibid.*, p. 10 B.

[36] "Carrefour de Buci fut longtemps lieu patibulaire; en 1621, una barrière, ou poste de 20 sergents, y fut établie..." (Rochegude et Dumolin, p. 532 f.).

night during the reign of Louis XIII, a period notorious for the ineffectiveness of police protection after dark.[37]

D'Audiguier's novels provide a number of interesting if often prejudiced observations on the social classes of the day. Most prominent, of course, are the nobility and lesser gentry, as would be expected in the writings of a poor but status-proud gentleman. The principal characters of all five novels are of noble birth, no matter how straitened or provincial their circumstances. Their class-consciousness and self-distinction from other groups is evident in Minerve's attempt to persuade Tatius to abandon his courtship of her; he is a jurist and townsman, she observes, whereas she was "née aux champs, et nourrie parmy la Noblesse";[38] as for his cultural background,

> estant nay dans la ville et nourry dans le Palais, il sçavoit mieux l'entretien d'un Juge avec ses parties, que les entregents et gentillesses accoustumées entre les Dames et les Cavaliers qui vivent aux champs.[39]

In *La Flavie*, Prince Belysare is at once impressed and puzzled by the grace, dignity, and courage of the young shepherd Pallante, qualities which are usually confined to the nobility. Before learning that he is actually Hector's son, Pallante himself is convinced that somehow he was intended for a more lofty station in life. "Ha! Tyrtée", he cries, "le Ciel nous devoit avoir faicts gentils-hommes, pour estre capables d'executer nos courageuses conceptions".[40]

D'Audiguier's gentlemen are usually enthusiastic warriors and duellists, many of whom seek military action in non-French campaigns in Hungary or in Holland to compensate for the dead calm of domestic tranquillity.[41] Even old Dorilas, Caliste's father, is

---

[37] See EMILE MAGNE, *La Vie quotidienne au temps de Louis XIII* (Paris: Hachette, 1942), pp. 42 ff.
[38] AUDIGUIER, *Les Diverses Affections*, p. 24 B.
[39] *Ibid.*, p. 33 A.
[40] AUDIGUIER, *La Flavie*, p. 21.
[41] "La noblesse française s'était toujours passionnée pour les aventures lointaines; le XVIe siècle, siècle de grands voyageurs, avait encore fortifié ce goût. D'autre part, certains de nos gentilshommes, peu portés vers les délassements intellectuels, souffraient de l'inactivité à laquelle la paix les avait réduits..." (REYNIER, *Le Roman sentimental*, 185 f.). "Ceux dont les es-

a veteran of Lepanto and other campaigns. In *Les Diverses Affections*, Adraste seems happiest when accompanying Louis XIII on military expeditions.

In keeping with actual practice of the period, the young courtiers in *Lysandre et Caliste* have received a superficial but fairly standard type of education for youths of their class.[42] It was provided largely by "académies" — male finishing schools of sorts, in which weapons training seems to have figured far more prominently than study.

The entertainment sought by d'Audiguier's gentlemen and ladies is in keeping with their leisure status. Apart from jousting, which by this time was primarily a literary convention rather than actual practice, walking and hunting appear to be their favorite outdoor pastimes. In the evening, they entertain one another at their town houses with dinners accompanied by music and by interminable conversation, which in these novels is usually flirtatious or teasing. In *Lysandre et Caliste*, protracted house-parties are held at country estates near Paris for the whole coterie of young couples and any of their relatives or friends who happen to be in the vicinity. On occasion, these assiduous courtiers attend balls and royal ballets at the Louvre. Their life becomes unusually animated at Carnival time:

> au temps de Caresme prenant...la saison semble obliger les François, et particulierement les Courtisans de donner la plus-part des jours à la foire, et la plus grande partie des nuits au bal...[43]

It is ironically realistic that although Lysandre occasionally composes music and poetry and writes copiously—just what is not clear—at his Mont Valérien hermitage, no other major character in these novels ever engages in any more intellectual occu-

---

prits ne peuvent vivre en oisiveté des armes eurent permission d'aller chercher de l'exercice en Flandre ou en Hongrie" (*Histoire de Henri IV*, par PIERRE MATHIEU; quoted in REYNIER, *Le Roman sentimental*, p. 186 n.).

[42] See MAURICE MAGENDIE, *La Politesse mondaine et les théories d'honnêteté en France, au XVIIe siècle, de 1600 à 1660* (Paris: Felix Alcan, 1926), I, 56 f.

[43] AUDIGUIER, *Aristandre et Cléonice*, p. 73.

pation than reading and writing love-letters, challenges, and replies to both. Intellectualism was not a salient trait of this class during d'Audiguier's lifetime. [44]

Contemporary religious practices are occasionally introduced into these novels, usually with deference. In *Lysandre et Caliste*, both rivals for Olinde's favor are moved by her dismissal to abandon the secular world, although unaware of each other's decision. Having become a Capuchin monk, Clairange is sincerely dedicated to his vocation and has no inclination to return to the torments of his former passionate existence, despite the insistence of his startled friends. He does manage to keep up with their activities for a time by means of a dispensation permitting him to visit Paris as a transient guest at a monastery there. Lydian, on the other hand, has a short-lived career as a preaching hermit at Montserrat. Despite his surprising homiletic skill which draws throngs of pilgrims, he is quickly induced to abandon this vocation upon learning of Clairange's withdrawal from competition for Olinde. His outspoken enthusiasm in returning to the secular world appears distressingly sacrilegious to both Clairange and Olinde. The only other clergyman portrayed by d'Audiguier is also a famous preacher, the monk Hiparque in *Aristandre et Cléonice*. He is one of the most interesting and least sympathetic characters in d'Audiguier's fiction, for his illicit passion for an admirer's wife causes him to degenerate into a violently lecherous hypocrite who is finally killed in self-defense by the object of his lust.[45]

D'Audiguier's characters are assiduous church-goers, at least in the contemporary Parisian setting of *Lysandre et Caliste* and *Les Diverses Affections*. No great religious fervor motivates them,

---

[44] See MAGENDIE, *La Politesse mondaine*, I, ch. iv. But it is incorrect to describe d'Audiguier as boasting of his own ignorance in *La Philosophie Soldade*, a misjudgment committed by PIERRE VILLEY, *Montaigne devant la postérité* (Paris: Boivin, 1935), p. 317. D'Audiguier in that work openly deplores his misspent formative years. In the 1614 edition of his *Oeuvres Poëtiques*, he lashes out at the anti-intellectual spirit prevailing among courtiers: "Car c'est grand cas que l'ignorance soit montée jusqu'à ce point, qu'en la Cour de France où les Lettres ont fleury jadis avec tant d'honneur, il faille rougir aujourd'hui de sçavoir escrire" (VITAL D'AUDIGUIER, *Oeuvres Poëtiques* [Paris: T. du Bray, 1614], Seconde Partie, "Au Lecteur").

[45] See Chapter V for a discussion of this character as Tartuffe's prototype.

however, for Mass is clearly a social event enabling them to meet and to be seen. Both Olinde and Minerve entertain their admirers and arouse jealous passions while ostensibly at worship. This social tendency probably results from the continuing integration of formal religion in daily life at the time.

Jurists appear in a generally unfavorable light in the fiction of this ex-magistrate. Due process of law is represented as inhuman persecution in *Lysandre et Caliste* when circumstantial evidence and perjury cast suspicion on Caliste during the investigation of her husband's murder. Incarcerated in the Petit Châtelet by judges "qui sont la pluspart semblables aux Chirurgiens, qui ne demandent que playes et bosses",[46] she is saved from condemnation and public execution in a carefully planned rescue from prison followed by a headlong flight from justice. This highly illegal procedure has only mild official repercussions,[47] and ultimately the case is removed from ordinary jurisdiction to be judged personally by Henri IV, whose legal thinking embraces such questionable techniques as trial by combat. In *Les Diverses Affections*, Senator Tatius is an esteemed member of the Parlement de Paris, a man whose skill in legal manipulation enables him to win Minerve's annulment suit as her attorney after she has already lost it "tout net plustot faute d'instruction que de droit".[48] Yet he is not above using her financial obligation to him as a means of legal coercion to win her hand. Nor does he hesitate later to compromise her status of legal separation from him with a possible pregnancy which he malevolently intends to disclaim.

Law enforcement officers also tend to be unattractive, even brutal figures. The morning after Caliste's escape, the warden of the Petit Châtelet awakens early, "comme c'est la coustume de telles gens, qui ne dorment jamais que quand le diable les berce".[49]

---

[46] AUDIGUIER, *Lysandre et Caliste*, p. 281.

[47] A remarkable incident occurred the year d'Audiguier first published *Lysandre et Caliste* and may well have inspired his Petit Châtelet episode: "En 1615, pendant le séjour de la Cour à Bordeaux, le cardinal de Sourdis, n'ayant pu obtenir, du Roi, la grâce d'un gentilhomme condamné à mort, attaquait la prison, faisait briser les portes, tuer le geôlier, et enlever le captif; l'affaire n'eut pas de suite" (MAGENDIE, *La Politesse mondaine*, I, 64).

[48] AUDIGUIER, *Les Diverses Affections*, p. 21 B.

[49] AUDIGUIER, *Lysandre et Caliste*, p. 341.

The archers escorting Caliste's bribed guard back to Paris are insolent but incompetent, and Lysandre has little trouble in dispersing them. In *Aristandre et Cléonice*, the well-intentioned fraud Tiribase is turned over to unsympathetic policemen, who "n'ont rien d'humain que le visage".[50] He is roughly handled by the arresting archers,

> qui font plus qu'on ne leur commande, et traittent indifferemment toute sorte de gens, sans sçavoir discerner les merites ny les qualitez des personnes.[51]

D'Audiguier's noble scorn for the prosperous bourgeoisie reveals itself obliquely in his portrayal of the wealthy old miser Philédas, who is unwilling to grant his daughter to the penurious but noble Tiribase and expresses contempt for the nobility's lack of aptitude in conducting business matters. But he nevertheless shows an awareness of social inferiority in his conviction that Tiribase would treat him as a valet rather than as a father-in-law, a sentiment which only Tiribase's proven assets and spectacular commercial success finally overcome.

An even less sympathetic picture is given of the Parisian lower classes. In order to establish a stake-out across the alley from Caliste's Petit Châtelet cell, Lysandre enlists the cooperation of a butcher's wife, "qui estoit femme, et davantage de Paris, et puis du commun qui se donneroit pour de l'argent...".[52]

He is amused by the ridiculous harangue of the butcher himself, "qui estoit un vray Parisien".[53] When Lysandre snatches Caliste's reply to his first message from the guard who has just intercepted it, he barely escapes from by-standers of "le menu peuple, levrier ordinaire du bourreaux".[54] Caliste's attendant Clarinde lacks the moral fibre which enables her noble mistress to resist sensual temptation. In *Les Diverses Affections*, Adraste's well-being is continually endangered by street gangs of robbers, Minerve's

---

[50] AUDIGUIER, *Aristandre et Cléonice*, p. 356.
[51] *Ibid.*, p. 367.
[52] AUDIGUIER, *Lysandre et Caliste*, p. 300. In *La Flavie*, he had spoken of "les ames basses et casanieres du populaire" (p. 2).
[53] *Ibid.*, p. 303.
[54] *Ibid.*, p. 310.

malevolent servants (corrupted by his rival), and even her drunken coachman. Her tenant farmer is described as "extremement brutal", "un vilain s'il en fust jamais, et plus meschant encore qu'il n'estoit vilain". [55]

Minerve's servants are typical of the unreliable and venal domestics appearing in these novels. Lysandre quickly buys the loyalty of Clarinde and a neighborhood woman for secret communication with Caliste at her country estate. Just prior to his duel with Cloridan, he is nearly poisoned by his incompetent cook, who carelessly substitutes hemlock for parsley while preparing dinner. Although Lysandre is fortunate to have a quick-witted Basque valet in his service, his Flemish valet is a dullard. Caliste's guard and serving-woman in prison are retained later as domestics, but their initial susceptibility to bribery is indicated as a weakness of their class. In *Les Diverses Affections*, Adraste's little English valet hides in a doorway drinking wine while his master is defending himself against attackers. Another valet —"un meschant laquay dont il avoit augmenté son train" [56]— decamps with his master's travel funds shortly before their scheduled departure for the La Rochelle campaign. In *Aristandre et Cléonice*, Tiribase's greedy valet is properly humiliated when he attempts to duplicate his master's luck by plunging into the well in which priceless jewels have just been discovered.

D'Audiguier's attitude toward non-compatriots is also reflected in his novels. In addition to his anti-Spanish bias, he is generally critical of outsiders. Foreigners invariably lose in any contest with Frenchmen, whether in Ancient Gaul, Henrician Paris, or Jacobean London, although d'Audiguier does praise the valor of English soldiers cooperating with the French as well as the incomparable beauty and spirit of English ladies in *Lysandre et Caliste*. Caliste's unwanted Frisian suitor Béranger is described as an "Aleman moins artificieux que naif", [57] and Minerve's beloved Arnoulphe appears as a tactless, boorish foreigner with none of the French social graces. Within France itself, d'Audiguier holds Parisians up to

---

[55] AUDIGUIER, *Les Diverses Affections*, p. 125 B.
[56] *Ibid.*, p. 124 A.
[57] AUDIGUIER, *Lysandre et Caliste*, p. 358.

ridicule in *Lysandre et Caliste*; in speaking of the failure of Caliste's parents to offer her asylum, he remarks,

> ce qui m'a fait souvent penser que ce n'est pas du tout sans cause qu'on dit que c'est une terrible nation que la normande. [58]

The early seventeenth-century attitude toward marriage and divorce is one of the most interesting aspects of *Les Diverses Affections*, for Minerve's marital difficulties are not in keeping with the stereotyped domestic bliss pervading d'Audiguier's other novels. [59] Conventionally enough, he had condemned parental coercion of daughters into marriage in *Lydamant et Callyante* and in *Lysandre et Caliste*; he now develops the theme with much realistic detail. Married at nine to an eleven-year-old, an incompatible union apparently never consummated, Minerve later goes to Paris as a very young woman to obtain a legal "séparation de corps et de biens". This amounts to an annulment in her case, possible for marriages contracted before puberty, which were often regarded merely as betrothals. [60] Soon after, she is coerced into marriage by her attorney Tatius. After bearing him two children in quick succession, she becomes exasperated with his boorishness and refuses to live with him. In Paris once again, she obtains a property separation, "bien marrie que deux enfants qu'elle en avoit l'empeschassent de se separer de corps". [61] During the remainder of the novel, she enjoys financial independence from Tatius, although on one unpleasant occasion she unwisely allows him to exercise his marital right.

Autobiographical details and allusions appear frequently. D'Audiguier, Sieur de la Menor, includes the name of his family estate in the title of his first novel, *La Flavie*. Several of his major characters are Gascons of gentle birth like himself: Prince Belsayre and

---

[58] *Ibid.*, p. 378.
[59] The problems of marriage and legal separation during this period are discussed in GUSTAVE FAGNIEZ, *La Femme et la société française dans la première moitié du XVIIe siècle* (Paris: J. Gamber, 1929), pp. 49-92.
[60] *Ibid.*, p. 59.
[61] AUDIGUIER, *Les Diverses Affections*, p. 35 A.

Princess Flavie, Lydamant (a Poitevin member of the Lusignan dynasty, which was driven out of Cyprus by the Turks in 1571), Lysandre, his parents, his sister, and his would-be fiancée Ypolite.

In addition to creating these attractive compatriots, d'Audiguier attributes much of his own background and personality to Minerve's suitor Adraste, noble but dependent for support on his father and Queen Marguerite, devoted to his King and royal policies, enthusiastic for military service, and unlucky in love.[62] Adraste's disapproval of Protestants and his satisfaction at their military and legal humiliation by Louis XIII are the same attitudes often expressed in d'Audiguier's own letters and discourses.[63]

D'Audiguier's lifelong obsession with the problem of duelling in a well-ordered society is apparent in all five novels. In *La Flavie*, Francus and Marthésie overcome and dispatch their foes in violent combat. Lydamant and Statyre cheerfully rout the challengers who seek to avenge the humiliation of the *châtelain*'s overly hospitable daughter; returning from Nicosye, Lydamant wrathfully overcomes his disguised friend Palémon to avenge an imaginary insult to Callyante's honor. Lysandre, Clairange, Lydian, and Alcidon risk legal reprisal by engaging in a four-man combat brought about by competition for Olinde's favor; Lysandre later kills Cloridan in another duel and is severely wounded himself; he nearly kills the disguised Ypolite in a duel as the result of her deliberate provocation during their chance encounter on the road to Paris. But Lysandre, aware of the social undesirability of the custom, is a reluctant participant in the first two of these duels, eloquently deploring the necessity of protecting his friendship and his honor in this way. By 1624, official disapproval of duelling was apparently so strong that Adraste never actually engages in it, although he attempts unsuccessfully to provoke several duels in spite of his friend's efforts at dissuasion. The interpolated story of Queen Marthésie's court in *Aristandre et Cléonice* portrays royal indignation at those who defy official injunctions against the custom. Aristandre himself jeopardizes his position at Court in this way but is quietly pardoned. The recurrence of the motif

---

[62] See Chapter V for a discussion of this largely autobiographical character.

[63] See ARDENNE DE TIZAC, Section IV ("Le Critique historique").

is understandable on the part of an author who felt strongly enough about the issue to write a lengthy historical and ethical treatise on it.

In *Lydamant et Callyante*, there appears a vigorous manifestation of d'Audiguier's bitterness arising from his precarious status as an unemployed soldier who has turned to literature for a living. Lydamant's guide on the Isle Volante tells of the rejection of honor and virtue by a practical, materialistic society which has substituted love and fortune as its idols. Those who persist in venerating the old ideals are regarded "avec un insuportable mespris, et une extreme indignation". [64] This overthrow of idealism has particularly affected gentlemen of merit but little means, like himself:

> On peut bien donner à un fol ou à quelque maquereau. Mais à un homme de bien, il y va de l'honneur de ceux qui l'auroient seulement pensé; quand il auroit versé tout son sang, et dépendu toute sa vie pour le service de son maistre. Qu'il soit vray, nous ne voyons presque rien icy que de pauvres gentilz hommes tous detaillez, qui ont une extremement bonne espee, qui ne leur sert que d'incommodité; d'autres qui ont la plume encore meilleure, et quelques uns qui ont l'espee et la plume tout ensemble, et ont rendu de certains treshonorables tesmoignages de l'une et de l'autre. Ausquels on n'a rien donné que de soubriquets, et de surnoms ridicules, qui leur ont fait desdaigner leur profession, et de laisser le mestier à des pauvres sots qui l'ont achevé de deshonorer.[65]

This is undoubtedly a true reflection of d'Audiguier's attitude toward his own difficult role in life. Seven years after the publication of *Lydamant et Callyante*, his situation had not changed, for the same bitterness of humiliation on the part of an author dependent on patrons and publishers is re-echoed in his *Oeuvres Poëtiques:*

> Que la sacré nom de Poëte autresfois si venerable et qui imprimoit tant de respect en la face et au cœur des hommes, soit un blasme; et ceux qui prennent tant de peine à honorer le monde, en reçoivent tant de mespris. La

---

[64] AUDIGUIER, *Lydamant et Callyante*, p. 125 A.
[65] *Ibid.*, pp. 128 Bff.

cause, à mon avis procede de leur pauvreté, car il n'est rien de si sot qu'un pauvre homme, et par consequent de si mesprisé; c'est ce qu'elle a de plus cruel et de plus injuste, de rendre ridicules ceux qui la souffrent. Et la cause de leur pauvreté vient du peu de soucy qu'ils ont de leur bien, cependant qu'ils enrichissent les autres de leurs tresors, lesquels estant ordinairement reconnus d'une ingratitude, il faut necessairement que le mépris soit un apannage des Muses. [66]

---

[66] AUDIGUIER, *Oeuvres Poëtiques,* Seconde Partie, "Au Lecteur."

CHAPTER V

CHARACTERIZATION

In a general way, d'Audiguier's characterization follows a pattern of development in keeping with that of his fictional technique during the course of his literary career. The characters of his early novels tend to be conventional, often stereotyped figures which show little originality of inspiration or portrayal. In the middle of his career, the characters of his novels are still primarily familiar types but are given a psychological elaboration which lends them a dimension of realism. His last two novels offer several characters of surprising freshness in their conception and treatment. As has been indicated, *Les Diverses Affections* was hailed by Küchler and von Wurzbach as one of the first French "realistic-psychological novels of character"; even amid the conventionality of *Aristandre et Cléonice* can be seen figures of notably original inspiration.

A. *La Flavie*. In this earliest and least original of d'Audiguier's novels, the heroine Flavie is portrayed as an ideal of unconditional, monochrome goodness. Flavie's consummate grace causes her to be surrounded by noble admirers at her mother's court; yet there is nothing of the coquette in her, as proved by her exclusive amorous affection for Francus. She is inflexibly virtuous, reacting with a proto-Victorian stuffiness to her cousin Martan's hesitant advances. His lust is resisted with an unsophisticated primness suggestive of a neglect of Flavie's social training by Queen Mathilde. Flavie's outrageous naïveté is demonstrated in her failure to see through Cousin Martan's abuse of their kinship in order to gain access to her intimate company as well as in her inability to recognize the peril involved in his suggestion that they stop off for the night at an inn instead of returning directly to the palace. Supernatural intervention in the form of a ghost is needed to warn her of that danger. She is ingenuous enough to assume that her rejection of Martan's advances will be dutifully accepted by him.[1] Her failure to appreciate Francus' jealous devotion and wounded pride is alarming enough to "les destins" for them to arrange a special supernatural revelation of the future for her so that she will not unwittingly jeopardize mankind's predestined felicity in centuries to come by discouraging his ardor.

Although Flavie's brother Belysare is represented only as a suitably amorous young prince, with valor and ambition appropriate to a grandson of Hercules, her suitor Francus reveals a few more traits in his two-dimensional portrayal. Having demonstrated great military prowess as the founder of the French kingdom, he now manifests noble jealousy (seen in his dignified withdrawal from Mathilde's court) in addition to unwavering devotion to his beloved. In attempting to rescue the kidnaped Flavie, he shows heroic courage in challenging Martan and his retinue of nearly thirty men. His search for her throughout Europe and Africa demands and receives unrelenting determination.

His subordinate companion Filamor is more interesting psychologically, for he harbors a secret passion for Flavie. Successfully resolving the conflict between love and duty in himself, he shows selfless dedication to restoring the happiness of Francus and Flavie in his ill-fated quest across Europe.

Belysare's cherished Marthésie is portrayed with little originality as a stock Amazonian warrior-maid in the Bradamante tradition. Loyal to her friends, she is swift to rush to the aid of Belysare's sister. She is a formidable opponent in her fearless, even aggressive attitude toward Filamor and the magician Merlan. Although not without humanity, she is pitiless in her wrath; her multiple sword-thrusts in slaying the defeated magician are tantamount to emptying a revolver when only one bullet is needed.

---

[1] As Flavie's kidnapers approach the Spanish frontier on the third day of her abduction, Martan demands her submission to him. "Ce fut lors que la Princesse s'apperceut un peu tard des infidelles desseins de ce Prince..." (AUDIGUIER, *La Flavie*, p. 78).

Her twin brother Pallante is a handsome adolescent whose noble bearing belies his humble pastoral occupation. Nevertheless, he is disquietingly immature, as is apparent in his whining complaints about wasting his life in an antipathetic environment, his petulant reproach to his guardian Tyrtée for withholding the revelation of the boy's true identity until this point, and his childlike oblivion of previous feelings and statements in his ultimate regret at abandoning the pastoral life. His youthful ardor compels him to leave at once to fulfill Cassandra's prophecy that he should one day refound Troy and crush Greece. This noble but woefully untrained youth thus plunges headlong into a military career. Although no further mention is made of him, it may be pessimistically (and unfairly) recalled that Troy was never refounded and Greece not crushed until the Roman conquest.

Flavie's cousin and abductor Martan is the most interesting character in the novel, thanks to the colorful wickedness the author delights in ascribing to a Spanish prince.[2] Not only is he lecherous, with unseemly designs on his own cousin's virtue, but also arrogant to challengers and vain in his resentment at Flavie's preference for Francus and her rejection of his own advances. He is crafty in scheming to gain her confidence and in using magic and false pretences in attempting to force her submission, which he hypocritically justifies as being of no danger to her honor under the circumstances. Finally, he is ruthless, untroubled by the the necessity of murdering Prince Perses to kidnap Flavie and cold-blooded in his determination to force her submission. His vindictive concealment of feelings and intentions is noted by d'Audiguier as typically Spanish behavior.[3]

B. *Lydamant et Callyante.* As d'Audiguier's closest approximation of the sentimental novel form, this work employs traditional motifs of the genre in its character portrayals. Of the three characters elaborated enough to reveal distinctly individual personalities, Callyante appears as a typical sentimental-novel heroine,

---

[2] "Ce gracieux entregent de Francus luy manque, et luy qui a plus d'artifice pour conduire un mauvais dessein, que de naïveté pour se faire aimer" (*ibid.,* p. 48).

[3] *Ibid.,* p. 63.

remaining outside the adventure-novel activity in which her lover Lydamant and his sister Statyre are involved.

Callyante is primarily accomplished as a court lady even though normally residing at a distant country estate. Lydamant is first attracted to her as a beautiful woman of exceptional social poise and conversational ability. In keeping with the extroverted social behavior required of successful courtiers in any age, she is an experienced coquette in her manner of dealing with male admirers, engaging in lengthy flirtation with Lydamant while retaining the devoted attention of the prince who introduced im to her. To facilitate her control of social situations at court and at home, she has developed the remarkably effective technique of appearing in the company of her sister Roxane; in this way, she is able to avoid unwelcome intimacies of conversation and conduct on the part of her suitors, dispensing with Roxane's presence only when she is prepared to accept such attentions.

Yet this flirtatious proclivity is accompanied by a stern moral conscience manifested in her sensitivity to any real or imagined compromise of her honor. Her feminine pride makes her react to possible social humiliation with the same compulsive severity. At the same time, she possesses a warmly affectionate nature, somewhat surprising in view of her other traits. In addition to her sensual responsiveness to Lydamant's boldly intimate caresses, her affection for him is apparent in her initial pleasure at his long visit to her father's estate. Although her despair at his reported death is abruptly followed by acceptance of another suitor's courtship,[4] she dedicates herself to him alone after the rival's unexpected death.

Lydamant is an almost schizophrenic combination of vigorous chivalric extrovert and passive, sighing lover of the sentimental-novel tradition. As a conventional chivalric hero, he is esteemed as a remarkably gifted soldier whose outstanding exploits prove

---

[4] "C'estoit neantmoins une fille en l'ame de laquelle les affections joyeuses, ou tristes, ne peuvent pas jetter de longues racines" (AUDIGUIER, *Lydamant et Callyante*, p. 5 A). "Et voyant que les choses faites ne se peuvent guerir que par l'oubliance, elle adjoute l'infidelité presente à l'ingratitude passée... Se reservant neantmoins un continuel pensement de se defaire de celuy qu'elle ne reçoit que par reverence des lois paternelles." (*ibid.*, p. 5 Bf.)

his courage in welcoming the physical danger of combat. His fearlessness is complemented by an impulsive quality which causes him to plunge almost blindly into situations where others might have paused for more prudent consideration, as in his furious assault on Palémon to avenge an imaginary insult to Callyante's honor. In keeping with the *Amadis* tradition, he demonstrates a hearty, amoral virility in his cheerful night-long cooperation with the *châtelain*'s passionate daughter.

Yet despite his apparent nerveless vigor, Lydamant is afflicted with the emotional immaturity of a sentimental-novel hero. Although eager for reconciliation with Callyante, he promptly worsens a strained situation in a childishly petulant scene, even putting the words of his dismissal in her mouth. On several occasions, he shows a deplorable lack of self-control under emotional stress despite the urgency of the situation. Estranged from Callyante at the outset of the novel, he weeps before going off to the Hungarian campaign and again after his return, hearing of Callyante's engagement to a rival. When a well-meaning innkeeper reminds him of this, he is unable at first to contain his rekindled grief. The sight of a misinformed and majestically wrathful Callyante near the end of the novel leaves him speechless and sighing piteously even though firm, swift action is desirable to determine and correct the obvious misunderstanding.

Like Callyante, he is highly sensitive to the disapproval of others. His avoidance of amorous competition seems to fall neatly into the psychological category of behavior called "leaving the field", for his consistent reaction is to withdraw rather than ride out storms of passion or submit to the humiliation of failure in his courtship. Like his beloved, Lydamant is adept at unflagging gallant conversation, no matter how trivial, a major pastime in a politely bantering society probably not unlike that of Marguerite de Valois' salon. With such poise, Lydamant is doubtless an ideal young courtier in the author's eyes.

Statyre is another of d'Audiguier's manifestations of the Bradamante Amazonian motif, which places such emphasis on exterior novelty as to admit of little portrayal of emotional states or psychological conflicts. Despite the physical strength which makes her masculine disguise irresistible to the *châtelain*'s frustrated daughter, Statyre's beauty and feminine grace are still perceptible enough to make her disturbingly attractive to Lydamant, who is understandably puzzled to find himself reminded of Callyante by this young and presumably virile knight. Although not really a professional Amazon, she never lacks confidence in her own military prowess, a self-assurance also apparent in her determination to carry out her mission of finding Lydamant. Although she demonstrates a remarkably calm sexual sophistication in maintaining her masculine disguise when importuned by the *châtelain*'s daughter and while discussing the incident later with Lydamant, she immediately regains a demeanor of girlish modesty upon resuming feminine dress and identity when safely back at her foster-father's home.

C. *Lysandre et Caliste*. In this modern adventure novel which still clings to the trappings of the novel of chivalry, the hero Lysandre is swiftly depicted in the opening pages as a model of stereotyped chivalric excellence. Second to none of his contemporaries in courtesy and valor, he is endowed with "l'ame toute libre, et toute guerriere, et le courage tout genereux".[5] As a result, he is unsurpassed in military skill, winning every duel and tournament in which he participates and suffering defeat only when trapped unarmed in an ambush. A more contemporary note appears in his mastery of the early seventeenth-century social graces, for he not only holds his own in salon conversation but also composes poetry and music, accompanying himself skillfully on the lute.

But this ideal young soldier-courtier suddenly finds himself overcome by an obsessive and highly unplatonic passion for Caliste, which he is never able to sublimate for long. Despite his perfidious ulterior motive in cultivating the intimate friendship of Caliste's husband Cléandre, he has the decency to be torn by a moral conflict between his love and his unwillingness to violate Cléandre's affectionate hospitality. However, Lysandre does violate it by making secret physical demands on Caliste in return for his notable services to her and to her family.

Such advances are the result of a certain irrational, brutal quality in him which is especially apparent in two vigorous but unsuccessful seduction attempts and in a violent tantrum of frustration after his second failure. This same trait has its final manifes-

---

[5] AUDIGUIER, *Lysandre et Caliste*, p. 4.

tation in the sensual enthusiasm with which he consummates his ultimate marriage.[6]

To his credit, he does appear to be less selfish after Cléandre's murder, for his rescue and subsequent protection of Caliste during their flight across Europe are not at the price of her submission, despite the favorable conditions arising from their enforced intimacy; instead, he is gallantly satisfied with "quelque legere faveur qui ne vaut pas le parler"[7] and her promise of eventual marriage. He is also unwavering in his devotion to her, despite the competition of Ypolite's great charms and the discouraging severity of Caliste upon attaining official vindication of her innocence. Not only strong and talented but also physically attractive and actively sensual, Lysandre is a hero in the sixteenth-century tradition of Amadis and Galaor, not in that of such fictional "honnêtes hommes" as Polexandre and Artamène, whose lofty and wholly spiritualized passion was soon to become *de rigueur* in composition for the novel-reading public of the second third of the seventeenth century.

Endowed with incomparable beauty and grace in the best chivalric tradition, Caliste is capable of winning any man's adoration, a dubious asset in view of the unwelcome, even dangerous attentions of her Frisian admirer Béranger and Lysandre's trial-by-combat challenger Lucidan. Fortunately, she is untainted by vanity and devotes herself unselfishly to her family and friends. Remarkably enough, one of her most conspicuous traits is an unabashed, candid sensuality; her unfeigned enjoyment of the physical aspect of marriage to Cléandre remains undiminished even after several years of their union. Although barely maintaining an ultimate propriety in her often compromising relations with Lysandre, she reveals this side of her nature again in deriving no less satisfaction than he from the transports of their wedding night.

Her virtue is precariously sustained through the application of an unreasonable legalistic morality which fails to take into ac-

---

[6] "Là les plus cheres faveurs de Caliste furent exposées au pillage, et à la fureur des jeunes desirs de Lysandre, qui voyant rangées à sa mercy tant de divines beautez qu'il avoit si religieusement adorées, se vengea sur elle de leur rigueur" (*ibid.*, p. 695).

[7] *Ibid.*, p. 354.

count the violence of Lysandre's passion. Having granted him a nocturnal rendezvous in her bedroom, where he finds her reclining alluringly and where he is forced to be a clandestine witness to an unforeseen hour of lovemaking by husband and wife, she is nonetheless outraged at his lustful advances after Cléandre's departure. In spurning his second attempt at seduction, she candidly admits his attractiveness in a blandly dispassionate statement:

> Contentez vous donc, que je n'ay pas moins de regret à vous imposer ceste loy, que vous mesme à la souffrir, et que la mesme passion que vous ressentez pour ne pouvoir obtenir ce que vous desirez illicitement de moy, je la ressens pour ne vous le pouvoir licitement accorder. [8]

Far from being promiscuous in bestowing her affection, Caliste is a model of decorum in the retiring modesty with which she avoids court society. She is doubtless sincere in her distress when her complaisance toward Lysandre has a corrupting effect on her morally unstable attendant Clarinde, a distress more lofty than mere concern at the implicit blackmail which results. In her grief at losing both Cléandre and her honor in one blow, Caliste is a genuinely pathetic figure, as is also the case when she falls gravely ill upon Lysandre's apparently final disappearance near the end of the novel. Even her jealous grief resulting from the rumor of Lysandre's affair with Ypolite can arouse a certain empathy, despite the exaggeratedly drastic schemes she devises to avenge herself.

Less attractive, though, are other manifestations of feminine irrationality, as for example her hesitation to accept Lysandre's help in escaping from prison because he is accused—even though falsely—of Cléandre's murder. Her temporary revulsion toward Lysandre when danger and dishonor are finally past is another instance of logically groundless behavior. Fortunately, she is capable of intelligent resourcefulness and discretion, which make possible her success in never arousing Cléandre's suspicion and in winning over her prison guard and attendant when informed of Lysandre's escape plan. Closer to the elegant heroines of the later *grands romans* than Lysandre is to their heroes, Caliste's person-

---

[8] *Ibid.*, p. 166.

ality remains more plausible than that of Alcidiane or Mandane because of those imperfections which d'Audiguier's unplatonic realism allowed to be portrayed in her character.

Cléandre is a much less complex figure than his wife. As Lysandre's closest friend and Caliste's devoted husband, he is a warmly affectionate, guileless young man, whose trust in those whom he loves is sheltered by an unreflective openness. In addition to conventional knightly valor in combat, his courage is also manifested in an indifference to danger in the haunted inn (surely more terrifying then than now) and in his unarmed encounter with the desperate Léon, caught intruding at night while venturing to keep an assignation with Clarinde. Although thoroughly dismayed at finding Lysandre's sword left behind by the unrecognized murderer, Cléandre never gives way to recrimination, dying as nobly as he had lived with a gracious farewell to Caliste. Sincerely generous, he has nothing of the ridiculously credulous near-cuckold in him.

Although a much less important figure, his brother Béronte is interesting for the irrational jealousy aroused in him by Cléandre's intimate friendship with Lysandre. Psychologically realistic in its motivation, his secret dislike is transformed into distrust when he learns of Lysandre's illicit passion for Caliste. Having been duped by Clarinde into believing that the affair had become flagrant, he is ready to believe Lysandre and Caliste responsible for Cléandre's murder. Because of his basically noble and generous nature, though, he can be made to realize and acknowledge the falsity of this charge when offered a rational explanation by earnest friends. It is true, however, that his later support of the fugitive pair is influenced by an increasing devotion to Lysandre's sister Ambrise. His courage and loyalty are never in doubt, for he is intended to be a sympathetic character.

Although Caliste's brother Lydian has much in common with his friend and rival Clairange, including education, travel, and passion for the fair Olinde, his impetuous and somewhat arrogant youthful ardor does not evolve into the fervor of a true religious vocation as does that of Clairange, who is moved by amorous frustration to abandon the world in favor of a calm, reflective life as a Capuchin monk. More favored in love than his rival (and thus spared the anguish of Clairange's jealousy), Lydian reacts to Olinde's dismissal in a more spectacular but less permanent way in becoming a famous preacher-hermit at Montserrat, where he spellbinds in impeccable Spanish while demonstrating a remarkable and hitherto unnoticed grasp of Christian theology. The news of his assured acceptance by Olinde quickly dissuades him from continuing in this role, and he immediately returns to his former life with its pleasures of jousting, duelling, and amorous gallantry. The insincerity of his temporary religious vocation is apparent in his sacrilegious conduct when reunited with his beloved. [9]

Olinde herself is an unusual woman in her unwillingness to commit herself publicly to either lover, although her preference for Lydian is made clear to both suitors in her midnight trysts with him while neither is supposed to call on her. This psychological quirk leads her to dismiss both suitors with an odd, oracular promise to accept the one who will be the latter to appear before her again. She does not appear to have foreseen the consequences of this hasty utterance, for their discouraged departure leaves her abandoned rather than relieved. His dilatory behavior is brusquely simplified in an eighteenth-century version of the novel, in which outright coquetry replaces indecision. [10]

As the willing choice of Lysandre's parents to be his bride, Ypolite is memorable for qualities other than her great beauty and inherited wealth. The last of the Amazons in d'Audiguier's prose fiction, she is the most remarkable of the three in view of her ability to captivate Henri IV and all his court with her ravishing feminine grace immediately after having fought for two full hours in a violent duel with the formidable Lucidan, whom not even Lydian had been able to defeat previously. Although strong-willed and aggressive in her efforts to defend her presumed suitor

---

[9] "Pardonnez moy Madame, disoit il, bien que je ne vous aye point offensée, sinon pour la penitence que j'ay faite, au moins pour la reverence de cet habit, que je viens jetter aux pieds de celle qui me la fait prendre" (*ibid.*, p. 235 f).

[10] "Jeune, riche et maîtresse de sa personne, elle vouloit éprouver le caractère de ses prétendans, peut-être jouir de leurs hommages: *la coquetterie est si adroite!*" ("Le Chevalier des Essars, et la comtesse de Berci" [condensation of Guillot de la Chassagne's reworking of d'Audiguier's *Lysandre et Caliste*], *Nouvelle Bibliothèque des Romans*, 2e année, V [Paris: 1799], 85). This source is hereafter referred to as *Nouvelle Bibliothèque*.

Lysandre, she is capable of gracious forgiveness despite the humiliation of finding herself rejected by him. By the affectionate withdrawal of her claim on him, she makes possible the joyous but still remote quintuple wedding which ends the novel.

As the most baleful of the few villains appearing in the novel, the fallen Clarinde is perhaps more to be scorned than pitied. Yet her moral downfall and subsequent vicious conduct deserve explanation if not pardon. D'Audiguier makes it clear that Clarinde's behavior had been acceptable up to the time Caliste took her into her confidence about Lysandre's attentions, although Lysandre had previously insured Clarinde's loyalty to his cause. It is Caliste's equivocal example of compromising behavior which leads to the corruption of her equally sensual but morally less firm attendant. Without this incentive, there would have been no occasion for Clarinde's tacit blackmail or for her later distortion of the truth when threatened with dismissal for flagrant immorality or with implication in Cléandre's murder. Her portrayal as an inherently vicious creature in a later version of the novel is a questionable over-simplification of her character.[11]

D. *Les Diverses Affections.* D'Audiguier's fourth novel offers none of the stereotyped characters of chivalric tradition which figure in his earlier works. Painstakingly contemporary in its setting and situations, lacking the devices seen in Lysandre's adventures "par ce que celles-là sont faintes, et celles-cy sont veritables",[12] this novel is without idealization or serious exaggeration in its portrayal of characters who are neither models of virtue nor incarnations of vice. Although artistically bleak and uneven, d'Audiguier's serious effort at psychologically realistic characterization provides a number of remarkably vivid insights which go far to redeem its experimental shortcomings. Whether or not this amounts to "a true artistic discovery, ... something entirely new in the French novel", as Küchler asserts,[13] is a matter of opinion;

---

[11] *Ibid.*, p. 70. Clarinde's role in Du Ryer's dramatization of the novel (1630) has been seen as that of "la première suivante de la scène française" (H. C. LANCASTER, "Pierre Du Ryer écrivain dramatique," *Revue d'histoire littéraire de la France*, XX (1913), 316.

[12] AUDIGUIER, *Les Diverses Affections*, "Advis au Lecteur."

[13] KÜCHLER, p. 95.

but it is certainly of scholarly interest. An examination of three principal characters will suffice to give an idea of the author's method.

D'Audiguier's Minerve is an unhappily married young noblewoman who obtains an annulment with great difficulty, only to find herself inmediately trapped into another unpleasant marriage. After driving away the second husband from his own bed and board, she finally emerges from this union with a legal separation, having been disqualified for another annulment by the birth of two children. Thus enjoying a degree of freedom without complete legal independence, Minerve can no longer properly offer encouragement to her suitors, a severe restriction for a selfish, calculating woman who has always taken advantage of the devotion of her numerous male admirers. [14]

Minerve appears almost neurotic at times in the inconsistency of her coquettish behavior. Her most deserving suitor, Adraste, finds himself her trusted confidant one day and an importunate guest the next. While making a great issue of her honor and virtue in repeated arguments with Adraste, she irrationally bestows her greatest affection on a rude, indifferent foreigner, Arnoulphe, whose callous boastfulness can only harm her reputation. Finding that calm, untroubled affection has no savor for her, she takes a perverse delight in playing off one admirer against another to arouse their jealousy: "... elle aymoit le haut goust en amour." [15] Yet despite her cavalier attitude toward Adraste, she is genuinely grieved at his angry withdrawals from competition and usually takes the initiative to convince him of her abiding affection; their

---

[14] "Minerve erscheint als ein die Männer unwiderstehlich anziehendes, kokettes, berechnendes, ihre Interessen geschickt pflegendes Weib. Also ein launenhaftes, nach Aufregungen und Sensationen in der Liebe verlangendes Weib, dem es eine Lust ist, sich leidenschaftlich begehrt zu sehen und sich mit feinen Worten zu verweigern, indem es sich halb gibt. Ein Wesen, das innerlich ganz unwahr ist, deren Element der Flirt, das listige Spiel, das Lavieren, Heucheln und Sichentschuldigen ist. Der Typus des schönen, die Sinne der Männer verwirrenden, aber sie immer nur hinhaltenden, nie sie befriedigenden, innerlich kühlen, äusserlich tugendhaften Weibes. Die geborene Liebesintrigantin, die geschickt ihren eigenen Instinkten zu gebieten weiss, stets eine Maske trägt, aber doch nicht über ihre wahre Natur zu täuschen vermag." (*Ibid.*, p. 93 f.)

[15] AUDIGUIER, *Les Diverses Affections*, p. 102 Bf.

final leave-taking is an equivocal bedroom scene lasting some fifteen hours.

An intelligent, spirited woman, she is nevertheless continually beset by the effects of her poor judgment in impetuous decisions. The result of having allowed herself to be trapped into a heavy financial obligation, her marriage to old Senator Tatius is doomed to failure. Her promise to underwrite part of his expenses for a seditious political venture has equally disastrous results. At the end of the novel, she is on the verge of being forced into dependence on Adraste's scheming rival Crassus, even though his method is essentially that used earlier by Tatius for the same purpose. She comes close to breaking off Adraste's courtship as the result of her failure to appreciate Crassus' insidious activity among her servants.

Her hapless suitor Adraste is a young soldier of limited financial means, dependent on his father's support and Marguerite de Valois' sporadic bounty. He is thus prevented from assuming a manner in keeping with his amorous passion and patriotic zeal. Despite the lack of any tangible reward for his military services, he is able to sublimate other concerns in his enthusiastic participation in Louis XIII's various campaigns of 1621.

Painfully sensitive to real or imagined slights and resentful of amorous competition, he is quick to withdraw to brooding solitude. Even when persuaded to resign himself to a subdued role as Minerve's friend and counselor, he longs to monopolize her affectionate attention. Although he is basically an upright, virtuous person, his overwhelming desire for Minerve leads him to rationalize shamelessly about "natural morality" and the propriety of secret caresses which avoid scandal.

An impetuous nature is manifested in his sudden decision to organize a serenade for the temporarily estranged Minerve as well as in his equally abrupt armed assault on a group of actors and jurists whom he mistakes for bandits. This trait is also apparent in the promptness with which he forgets the past when shown affection; both Minerve and her rival Cariclée discover this in learning that he is capable of amorous distraction.

The most interesting aspect of Adraste's character is its autobiographical parallel with the personality of d'Audiguier, an impetuous, often penurious gentleman-soldier and protégé of Queen Marguerite, a passionate man whose courtship of women fell short of gratification and whose greatest satisfaction appeared to be found in vigorous but unrewarding military service, notably in the same 1621 campaigns.[16] In view of the circumstances of d'Audiguier's murder soon after he wrote this novel, it is particularly ironic to read of Adraste, "C'estoit un bon joueur, mais il ne se servoit pas bien des chances".[17]

Although described in considerably less detail, the rather pathetic figure of Minerve's old and unloved second husband Tatius shows d'Audiguier's sustained attempt at realism in this novel. Even though Tatius is intended to be an unsympathetic character, much of his offensive behavior can be traced to normal and understandable motives. Passionately in love with Minerve, he unhesitatingly sacrifices his legal career in order to conform to her social status. The use of financial blackmail to achieve his desire is unwise but incidental to his otherwise honorable intention. Her resentment at being forced into such a marriage probably does much to render him a boorish and ill-tempered mate, as do the reduced means resulting from his professional retirement. Other actions of his which indicate unsound judgment include his voluntary implication in a disloyal political scheme and his tricking Minerve into sexual relations with him after their legal separation. Properly resented by her, this last spiteful deed seems to be a man-

---

[16] The autobiographical nature of this novel was exploited by Barwick, who entitled his English translation *Love and Valour: Celebrated in the person of the Author, by the name of Adraste. Or, The divers affections of Minerva*. Barwick also fabricated a second part in keeping with d'Audiguier's unfulfilled promise to write one: "Divers amorous Epistles wrote by the Author to the same Lady, during the time mentioned in the precedent story, and not therein spoke of" (*ibid.*, p. 123). Barwick's familiarity with the circumstances of d'Audiguier's murder seems apparent in an editorial comment in this new section: "The next epistle he wrote unto her, is the last mentioned in the story, where wee leave him departed for the Army, from whence having sent her sixe or seven severall Letters before he received one backe, being returned to *Paris*, hee wrote the following Epistles, which may give much light to the Reader, of the argument of the second part that was neer finished, but could not wholly, for that, what the Author intended otherwise (as may be thought) fill out an unhappy tragedie signed with his owne lives bloud, after he had foure or five times victoriously returned out of the field on severall appeals, honoured with the better on his enemies, by whom he was unfortunately murthered, neer the bed-side of this Lady" (*ibid.*, p. 163).

[17] AUDIGUIER, *Les Diverses Affections*, p. 6.

ifestation of his thwarted, humiliated passion rather than of any fundamental malice.

E. *Aristandre et Cléonice*. After the unusual contemporary realism of *Les Diverses Affections*, the characterization of this novel is relatively insignificant, with a few exceptions of surprising importance. In *Aristandre et Cléonice*, d'Audiguier emphasizes petty court intrigue rather than character analysis in the main plot. If Sorel is correct in his assertion,[18] the incidents of this main plot are thinly disguised situations actually arising at Louis XIII's court, which would have discouraged any inventive analysis of the personalities involved as well as any elaboration of fictional detail.

The handsome young courtier Aristandre appears to spend most of his time devising ways to win, recover, or conceal the affection of Cléonice, succeeding in overcoming every obstacle except the ultimate decision of the monarch himself that he should marry another woman. In view of his previous emphatic vows of fidelity to Cléonice, Aristandre is hard put to justify his prompt submission to *raison d'Etat* but offers a bland explanation appropriate to such a puppet courtier.

Cléonice is equally unrealistic as a model lady-in-waiting who seems to have little else to do except cooperate in Aristandre's schemes for unauthorized communication with her or impose temporary exile on him to punish real or imaginary offenses. She is most plausible in her grief and humiliation when Aristandre is finally compelled to renounce his loyalty to her.

The basic motivation of their implacable foe, the busybody chief lady-in-waiting Arsilée, is never quite certain, for her stereotyped role as a vindictive storyteller is not developed beyond the conventional model for it. Her character is enigmatic but forceful enough in her long though fruitless campaign to turn the complaisant Queen against the young couple.

In the third interpolated story of this novel, d'Audiguier portrays a valiant young knight, Tissaferne, whose selfishness and arrogance seriously embarrass Queen Marthésie and ruin the careers of those who have befriended him. His insolent disrespect

---

[18] Sorel, *L'Anti-Roman*, II, 970.

for the moral standards of the Queen's palace —even though he is under house arrest there— results from a stubborn persistence in gratifying his amorous passion for Silésie. His engaging in a duel in the palace garden constitutes flagrant defiance of royal authority which prohibits the practice.

It is d'Audiguier's first interpolated story, however, which provides the most notable characterization in the entire novel. This tales of a respected clergyman's criminal passion for the wife of his greatest admirer was identified some thirty years ago as Molière's probably source for the characters of Tartuffe, Elmire, and Orgon.[19] This revelation by two scholars working independently of each other is all the more gratifying in view of the editorial lament found in the "Grands Classiques" edition of *Tartuffe*: "On ne saura jamais ... d'où est parti le trait de lumière qui a tout à coup frappé le génie."[20] The essential elements found in both works are too numerous to be coincidental. Molière's transformation of Hiparque into a pious layman is of course a late development in his composition of the play, made necessary by clerical opposition to its initial version, *L'Imposteur*, in which the villain was still a clergyman.

What is striking, however, is the way in which Molière's artistic skill was able to improve the situation and characters furnished by d'Audiguier through subtle modification. The somewhat passive outraged virtue of Eurigène becomes an understanding and clever exploitation of her would-be seducer by Elmire. The hesitant Orgon is more capable of investigative action than his apathetic prototype Licidas, who persists in a calm incredulity despite his wife's urgent warnings. Originally a genuinely devout monk who degenerates into an impatient lover over a four-month period, Hiparque is less cunning in his seduction campaign than Tartuffe, a thorough rascal from the first who stalks his prey with careful

---

[19] MAGENDIE, "Une 'source' inconnue du *Tartuffe*"; H. JACOUBET, "Sources," *Annales de l'Université de Grenoble* (N. S.), XVIII (1941), 247-257. In acknowledging Magendie's earlier discovery, Jacoubet points out a somewhat different presentation in his own article, prepared before he learned of Magendie's note on the same subject (*ibid.*, p. 254).

[20] Quoted in MAGENDIE, "Une 'source' inconnue du *Tartuffe*," p. 930 f.

circumspection.[21] Some of Hiparque's arguments are no longer suitable for use by Tartuffe in view of Elmire's considerable intelligence; she obviously could not be taken in by such a transparent ploy as Hiparque's shamelessly unsubtle distinction between the intention of his preaching and that of his own practice. As Molière's villain speaks, "la passion gronde sous ces métaphores dévotes, et la flamme fait fondre l'onction".[22]

A further improvement is seen in Molière's postponement of the second interview between pursuer and pursued until after Orgon has been warned. Whereas no intervening psychological change occurs in d'Audiguier's version, this scene becomes much more interesting in Molière's; for Elmire is now obliged to be as skillful as possible in attempting to unmask her wary admirer, who has barely escaped exposure already. Hiparque's use of a charm to neutralize Licidas and the servants at the crucial moment is replaced by wholly psychological motivation for Orgon's lack of vigor, a modification which demonstrates Molière's care in preserving that continuity of character for which he is celebrated.

D'Audiguier offers a violent conclusion in which Eurigène, forced to kill her seducer with his own dagger, tosses Hiparque's body into the street and is quickly vindicated by the police, who conceal the affair in an effort to preserve the esteem in which the local clergy was held. Such a *dénouement* was impossible for Molière in view of clerical sensitivity to unfavorable portrayal in the 1660's. His own concern for *bienséance* would also have made its use unlikely; the contrived ending of *Tartuffe* which depends on royal omniscience to resolve the problem is necessarily less effective.

Commenting on the difference in conception between the two authors, Jacoubet remarks,

---

[21] "Ce ne fut pas sans un grand combat qu'il se laissa vaincre à sa passion..." (AUDIGUIER, *Aristandre et Cléonice*, p. 32); "...la seule pensée de son crime le faisoit rougir: et celuy qui parloit si hautement devant tout le monde, n'osoit pas soupirer un seul mot devant une femme" (*ibid.*, p. 34).

[22] MAGENDIE, "Une 'source' inconnue du *Tartuffe*," p. 936.

> Vital d'Audiguier est un homme d'épée, aux aventures jusqu'à la fin comprise, tragiques: il écrit un roman; Molière, un bourgeois, traite le sujet en comédie. [23]

This neat, rather facile generalization appears to be exceptionally apt.

---

[23] JACOUBET, p. 253.

Chapter VI

EVOLUTION OF FORM AND STYLE

It would be futile to attempt to trace a clear-cut pattern of the development of form throughout d'Audiguier's career as a novelist. Such an effort would merely prove that it is impossible to impose a system of logical regularity on this impetuously opportunistic author. The one area of evolution worth noting in this respect is a general trend away from a cautious conformity in using traditional motifs and devices to a more original selection and adaptation of them—and ultimately to the use of more personal and relatively experimental elements in their place.

Of the five novels published between 1606 and 1625, it is d'Audiguier's first which best reflects the neophyte's anxious cleaving to fictional conventionality. *La Flavie* represents an effort to exploit two literary traditions at the same time, unfortunately without blending its epic and pastoral elements in a homogeneous whole. As was indicated in Chapter III, his use of Ancient and Renaissance epics in this novel usually amounts to direct imitation rather that adaptation, as in the vision of future kings and in the closing scene of the magician's death. Such fidelity occasionally results in the use of expressions lifted directly from d'Audiguier's eminent sources. *La Flavie's* Thracian pastoral scene is equally imitative in its representation of the Arcadian setting, the shepherds, their diversions, and even their food. D'Audiguier's language in this episode differs from that used elsewhere in the novel, for at this point it is laboriously evocative of the traditional Arcadian idyll.[1]

It is significant, however, that this pastoral episode is not only secondary in *La Flavie* but also unique in all d'Audiguier's novels. Pastoral fiction prior to *L'Astrée* was not a thriving genre, for the noble society of Henri IV's reign seems to have preferred idealized portraits of itself amid its ordinary surroundings. The stylized, oblique portrayal offered by the pastoral device was primarily restricted to the theatre at this time — a tendency fortified by Italian influence — whereas the novel was regarded as a more suitable vehicle for a type of realism which was almost as stylized as the pastoral itself.[2] The success of *L'Astrée* does not appear to have encouraged novelists to revitalize the pastoral novel; in addition to discouraging competition with such a masterpiece, d'Urfé's complicated web of several genres was a departure from the slender traditional structure of such fiction.

Published only a few months after *La Flavie*, *Lydamant et Callyante* is an attempt to capitalize on the popular taste for novels depicting an idealized modern French setting. D'Audiguier's work is again a hybrid, like others of the period, incorporating situations and language associated with the flourishing sentimental novel but providing an episodic series of adventures in imitation of the sixteenth-century novel of chivalry. Military service abroad, single and group combats, eventful journeys, and perilous sea voyages are typical of this sort of fiction, which was savored by the restless noble class vegetating in the peaceful conditions of Henri IV's reign; d'Audiguier provides them all. Yet he is occasionally obliged to hurry his travelers on to their destinations in order to maintain Lydamant's languishing courtship of the relatively stationary Callyante.

D'Audiguier shows considerably more self-confidence in his handling of this second novel. In addition to its conventional sentimental and chivalric elements, *Lydamant et Callyante* contains scenes which a more timid author might not have attempted. The forthright bawdiness of the episode involving the *châtelain*'s

---

[1] An example of this is cited in Chapter III (Prince Belysare's first sight of the shepherds' flocks).
[2] See REYNIER, *Le Roman sentimental*, pp. 195 ff.

daughters is relatively commonplace in novels of the *Amadis* tradition, but it is startling to find in a novel where love is elsewhere represented as a spiritualized passion requiring great circumspection in achieving its concrete physical goal.[3] Even more remarkable is the Isle Volante episode, for bitter social satire is not characteristic of the traditional adventure novel, in which a pretence of reality is maintained. The thinly veiled autobiographical complaints voiced by Lydamant's guide are surprising on the part of an author whose literary career has just begun. In this episode, although not original in its inspiration, d'Audiguier momentarily turns from stringing together conventional motifs to make a personal and presumably sincere observation about the difficulties suffered by gentlemen of his own station and qualifications.

During the eight years elapsing between the publication of *Lydamant et Callyante* and that of *Lysandre et Caliste*, the political stability imposed on France by Henri IV was shattered by his assassination and the subsequent grasping for power by the nobility during Louis XIII's minority. With this atmosphere of civil war came a popular craving for adventure rather than sentimentality in fiction, a shift which favored the restoration of the reversals and supernatural elements of the Byzantine novel.[4]

These circumstances resulted in d'Audiguier's composition of a fictional *tour de force* in *Lysandre et Caliste*. Over twice as long as any other novel of his, this work shows a very different handling of the same basic fusion of contemporary scene and chivalric adventure used in Lydamant et Callyante. Seventeenth-century Europe is represented with considerably greater precision, as is also true in references to contemporary Parisian buildings and streets. The linear series of adventure episodes in *Lydamant et Callyante* is replaced by the progression of a whole set of concurrent events, accompanied by a wealth of incidental detail and the frequent observations of an omniscient author.

---

[3] D'Audiguier's episode seems to have been savored by the reading public, for it was later used by DU VERDIER in *Le Chevalier hypocondriaque* (*ibid.*, p. 184 n.)

[4] REYNIER observes that this vogue probably explains the four editions of d'Audiguier's revision of Amyot's Heliodorus which were published between 1609 and 1623 (*ibid.*, p. 351 f.).

The hasty composition of *Lysandre et Caliste* is especially apparent in the awkward padding of Books IX and X (comprising over a quarter of the work), which arrests the fair momentum attained in the earlier chapters. This final chain of unnecessary reversals serving only to protract the novel—thereby delaying its obvious conclusion—is probably the weakest artistic aspect of *Lysandre et Caliste*. From a structural standpoint, the novel should have ended with the official vindication of the protagonists' innocence and the punishment of the guilty Léon and Clarinde. Instead, another reversal occurs which leads to the Mont Valérien episode and sixty more pages to traverse before the inevitable marriage scene concluding the work.

On the other hand, the interesting phychological portrayal of several characters and the degree of suspense achieved in the jailbreak episode are certainly to d'Audiguier's credit as a novelist. More important from the standpoint of literary history is the imitation of Cervantine episodes found in this novel, for d'Audiguier is one of the first of many French authors to exploit *Don Quixote* and the *Novelas exemplares*.

Although the nine-year period following the publication of *Lysandre et Caliste* was without further original fiction on d'Audiguier's part (except for the *récit* of his lackey's "conversion" in 1623), the great variety of his literary production during this time doubtless had a maturing effect on his technique and style as a novelist.[5] His translation of two Spanish picaresque novels (*Marcos de Obregón* and *La Desordenada Codicia de los bienes ajenos*) appears to have been particularly significant in the composition of his most original novel, *Les Diverses Affections* (1624). Although retaining the contemporary-scene convention, he discards many traditional devices in his effort to create an illusion of unvarnished realism in portraying the problems and behavior of his characters. His unattractive but authentic picture of night-time Paris includes street brawls with helpless actors as well as with dangerous criminals in scenes of picaresque cynicism. References to Adraste as

---

[5] It was written in six months, of which over three were spent convalescing from sword wounds, according to d'Audiguier, who also laments the lack of proofreading before the publication of the novel (*Lysandre et Caliste*, "Advertissement au Lecteur").

a knight are usually ironic to the point of satirizing traditional chivalric motifs,[6] an impression furthered by Adraste's anti-climactic difficulties of illness and lodging problems during Louis XIII's military campaign, as well as the futility of his eager pursuit of non-existent rebels while en route to Normandy. His inability to provoke duels also has a parodic quality, although the author's deference to official discouragement of the practice is probably a more significant factor.

D'Audiguier's previous emphasis on adventure is now greatly modified, for most of the incidents occurring in *Les Diverses Affections* are singularly unheroic events. He concentrates instead on the establishment and inter-action of unconventional characters, whose direct or indirect autobiographical inspiration contributes greatly to the realistic quality of the novel. It is, in fact, this inspiration which makes the extent of d'Audiguier's skill in psychological analysis uncertain here, despite the later praise of Küchler and von Wurzbach for his literary pioneering in this respect. In view of the lack of a true second part of *Les Diverses Affections*, together with the translator Barwick's reference to d'Audiguier's murder,[7] it appears that this novel may not have taxed d'Audiguier's inventiveness as much as his skill in compiling personal experiences and attitudes in a fictionalized pattern.

Anyone hoping to find a consistent linear evolution in these novels from the conventional and imitative to the original and experimental would be chagrined at coming upon *Aristandre et Cléonice*, apparently written at approximately the same time as *Les Diverses Affections*. As a frame novel, it is a throw-back to a literary convention antedating the novel of chivalry and even the *Decameron* tradition, for the use of a vindictively ax-grinding storyteller is one of the oldest fictional devices. Its pseudo-Persian setting disguising contemporary personalities and situations at Court is an artifice which was not without criticism at the time[8] and which resulted in a magnification of exceptionally trivial incidents

---

[6] For example, the title "Chevalier au cœur my-parti" given him by his two *maîtresses* and the promised guerdon which Minerve does not have time to make before his departure at the end of the novel.

[7] See the discussion of the character Adraste in the preceding chapter.

[8] See Sorel, *L'Anti-Roman*, II, 970.

of gallant intrigue — hair-filching, exchanging or betraying love-letters, distracting unfavorable attention, and the like.[9]

The interpolated stories, however, are to d'Audiguier's credit as attempts at brief fiction, for of the four only the story of Tiribase falls back into the needlessly protracted, episodic looseness of *Lysandre et Caliste*'s last chapters. Although the story of Queen Marthésie and the arrogant young Tissaferne has relatively little suspense in its portrayal of the evil effects of pride, ingratitude, and royal complaisance, it has an interesting topical quality suggestive of actual situations involving Marie de Médicis. As an entertaining adaptation of a venerable motif, the "Marriage to a Statue" story is narrated concisely in vigorous and colorful language. In the most remarkable story of the four, that of the hypocritical preacher-monk Hiparque and his victims, d'Audiguier provides what is probably the most original as well as most successful episode in all his fiction. Although there are shortcomings of motivation and plot development (later eliminated by Molière),[10] this description of the moral degeneration of a leading religious figure is unforgettable, as are the desperate efforts of his principal victim to elude and yet expose him. Despite their interest, however, the interpolated stories are considerably longer and more elaborate than justified by their context in the main plot; their lack of relevance drew jeers from Sorel soon after the novel was published.[11]

---

[9] "Que l'on me permette encore de rapporter icy une faute de jugement qui est dans ce livre; l'Autheur dit ces paroles; *Cleonice promit à Arsilée non seulement de ne voir jamais Aristandre, quoy que ce fust au plus loin de sa pensée, mais aussi de ne suivre jamais autre volonté que la sienne. La promesse estoit equivoque, car elle pouvoit entendre la volonté d'Aristandre, ou d'Arsilée, ou la sienne propre; aussi l'avoit-elle faite avec intention de ne la point tenir.* L'equivoque est bonne dans ce discours que fait l'Autheur, mais elle ne pouvoit pas avoir lieu dans le discours parlant à Arsilée; Il faloit qu'elle luy dist, je vous promets de ne voir jamais Aristandre, et de ne suivre jamais autre volonté que la vostre; tellement que Daudiguier a fort mal raporté ceste chose, et voulant faire une petite finesse, s'est aussi lourdement trompé que fit jamais aucun escrivain." (*Ibid.*, p. 971 f.)

[10] For modern critical opinion on this matter, see the discussion of Hiparque in the preceding chapter.

[11] "C'est tousjours une mesme Dame qui les raconte à la Reyne de Perse sur ce qui se presente, et pour vous monstrer que cela est forcé, cette Reyne se rit mesme de l'humeur de cette Dame qui veut tousjours conter quelque histoire" (SOREL, *L'Anti-Roman*, II, 970).

Although the evolution of d'Audiguier's form can be seen only in a very general way, it is possible to determine a perceptible change in his style and language during the period in wich his novels were first published. An initial cleaving to that inflated, pompous writing known as the "style Nervèze" quickly gave way to an increasingly direct style, which is relatively devoid of traditional ornamentation in his last novels.

Simplicity of expression was not usually a literary goal at the time *La Flavie* and *Lydamant et Callyante* were published.[12] The ponderous simile and Petrarchan metaphor were not to be ignored by novelists who tried to be sensitive to popular taste. In concocting the prose of *La Flavie*, d'Audiguier does not shrink from comparing the entry of love into Filamor's heart to that of the Trojan Horse into Troy. To indicate that a scene takes place in autumn, he resorts to an elaborate circumlocution:

> C'estoit en la saison que la belle Eleusis tond au Soleil les blonds cheveux de la terre, et que les champs, orgueilleux de leurs riches fertilités, invitent tout le monde à jouyr de leurs delices.[13]

Francus' Turkish horse, "faisoit ardre ses yeux hors de la teste, comme deux astres qu'on luy eust attachés au front".[14] Wary of Martan's lecherous conniving, Flavie "ne s'endormit pas fort au doux oreiller de ses paroles".[15] When she looks at her would-be seducer, his eyes are immediately blinded by hers, "dont les benins regards lui courent en frissonnant par le corps, comme un esclair de tonnerre".[16] Her "poitrine desbraillée" half exposes her breasts, "d'où sortoyent une infinité de beaux et jeunes Amours, qui halei-

---

[12] "Als ein Ergebnis der preziösen Gesellschaft unter Heinrich IV. hatte er [the sentimental-adventure novel] die Eigenart, die einfachsten Gedanken in einen gesuchten, mit Metaphern und Hyperbeln überladenen Stil zu kleiden, und dadurch die natürlichen Gefühle unwahrscheinlich und schablonenhaft zu machen" (KARL BICHLMAIER, *Die Preziosität der sentimentalen Romane des Sieur des Escuteaux* [Wertheim a.R.: Bechstein, 1931], p. 13).
[13] AUDIGUIER, *La Flavie*, p. 16.
[14] *Ibid.*, p. 37.
[15] *Ibid.*, p. 58.
[16] *Ibid.*, p. 65.

nans l'air, parfumoyent gratieusement sa circonference de souëfves respirations". [17] Her hair shines in the lamplight "comme lames de fin or bruny pendantes au vent, et branlantes contre le Soleil". [18] Her eyes, "plus estincellans que l'acier embrasé, qu'on forge sur l'enclume, jettent les esclairs et les foudres en telle abondance que Martan s'en estonne, et souffre cependant en son ame une combustion inextinguible". [19] The providential appearance of Francus when Flavie's virtue is most imperiled affords d'Audiguier an opportunity to insert a ponderous conceit:

> Ses armes reluisent à l'envy des flambeaux celestes, et du plombeau de son espée sort une clarté lumineuse qui luy faict jour à toute heure de la nuict. [20]

Although written soon after *La Flavie*, *Lydamant et Callyante* offers far fewer examples of such pompous eloquence. On the other hand, antithesis now appears as a conspicuous device. Callyante's eyes resemble both lightning and the sun; they are also the comet of Lydamant's misfortune and the star of his happiness. When he "acoste...céte inacostable", [21] his eyes are opened by her beauty and blinded by her love, for even "les plus froids courages" among her suitors burn with desire and even the most ardent desires are chilled by "la grandeur de son courage". [22] She forces admirers to die and yet to live; her words inspire fear, yet her looks arouse hope. Lydamant's courtship is jeopardized by her "trop vray depart...et le trop faux rapport qu'on luy fit de [Lydamant]". [23] Upon returning from Hungary, he is greeted "d'une triste joye" [24] by his friend Palémon. An innkeeper's jovial comment on Callyante's engagement to another suitor has a violent

---

[17] *Ibid.*
[18] *Ibid.*, p. 66.
[19] *Ibid.*
[20] *Ibid.*, p. 85.
[21] AUDIGUIER, *Lydamant et Callyante*, p. 41 B.
[22] *Ibid.*, p. 36 B.
[23] *Ibid.*, p. 48 A.
[24] *Ibid.*, p. 7 A. D'Audiguier's use of this expression is defended by Antoine Adam: "...au nom de quelle fausse idée de la simplicité du style pourrait-on juger son expression ridicule?" (ADAM, I, 107).

effect on Lydamant, described in what is probably d'Audiguier's most notorious passage:

> A le voir pleurer, on eust dit qu'il estoit tout d'eau, et par ses soupirs il temoignoit n'estre rien que vent. Au dehors ce n'estoit que terre, au dedans ce n'estoit que feu, qui presidant en son interieur en chassoit les qualitez qui luy sont contraires. [25]

Lysandre et Caliste provides several examples of inflated style, but these are relatively infrequent in proportion to the unusual length of the novel. Caliste, accompanied by other ladies, is described as a moon among stars; the same ladies are later referred to as planets at Court — "un Ciel bien serein semé de clairs Astres, dont leurs Majestez estoient les principaux luminaires". [26] Lysandre is credited with several metaphorical accomplishments. Although a lion in the street brawl outside the Petit Châtelet, he is a stag in his escape from the crowd. When he weeps, he makes "une autre Seine de ses larmes"; [27] when he sings, his love inflames "les deïtez de la Seine, et les mesmes glaces dont sa riviere estoit alors prise". [28] The "claires ondes" of the Thames are troubled by the noise of Lysandre's combat, during which a flock of birds is killed on the wing by a great shout from the crowd below. [29]

The greatest stylistic weakness of this novel, however, does not lie in such conceits. As was suggested earlier, it is found in d'Audiguier's artless stringing together of episodes in the last two chapters with the apparent intent of lengthening the novel without making organic changes in his plot. [30] There is no lack of further evidence of negligent composition, which is especially apparent in his repetition of particular phrases and expressions. On at least twenty

---

[25] AUDIGUIER, *Lydamant et Callyante*, p. 48 A. This passage is cited as an example of the most ridiculous and tasteless writing of the period in Reynier, *Le Roman sentimental*, p. 334.

[26] AUDIGUIER, *Lysandre et Caliste*, p. 562.

[27] *Ibid.*, p. 634.

[28] *Ibid.*, p. 655.

[29] *Ibid.*, p. 469.

[30] One particularly tedious passage is followed by this remark: "Ceste longue harangue achevee avec une incroyable patience de leurs Majestez..." (*Ibid.*, p. 686).

occasions d'Audiguier openly declines to elaborate upon scenes and conversations which he mentions in the course of his hasty narration; these evasions are expressed in monotonously similar formulas of apology or self-justification.

Les Diverses Affections is remarkably free of "style Nervèze" conceits.[31] Although uneven and monotonous, its prose has a directness which often assumes the form of ironic observation far removed from the ponderous idealization common in the earlier novels. The trivial nature of most of its incidents—perhaps stemming from the realism of autobiography—is partly responsible for the plodding and often tedious development of its uncomplicated plot.

An impression of stylistic retrogression in *Aristandre et Cléonice* is conveyed at the outset by a passage which would have been appropriate in one of d'Audiguier's first novels:

> La premiere fois qu'Aristandre ouvrit les yeux sur ceste beauté, il l'aborda tout de flamme, et la trouva toute de glace; mais ceste froideur fit un effet tout contraire à sa qualité, car au lieu de le refroidir, elle l'alluma davantage: Soit que Cleonice eust la proprieté de la neige, comme elle en avoit la blancheur, qui brusle les plus hauts lieux qu'elle touche: soit qu'Aristandre eust celle du feu, qu'un extreme froid rend plus violent.[32]

After this alarming beginning, however, the novel returns to the directness of style found in *Les Diverses Affections*.[33] As in that earlier novel, the reduction of adventure to day-by-day trivialities —in this case, of the bantering conversations and flirtations of seventeenth-century French courtiers—makes it difficult to sustain an interest in their recital, although the recurrent motif of nascent royal absolutism offers some incentive to continue.

---

[31] The two sole examples of the earlier, more flowery language occur at the beginning and at the end of this novel. Minerve's beauty "luy acquist plustost des Esclaves que des Juges" (AUDIGUIER, *Les Diverses Affections*, p. 4 A); in the final bedroom scene, "Minerve auparavant plus cruelle qu'une Lionne estoit devenue plus douce qu'une Colombe" (*Ibid.*, p. 144 A).

[32] AUDIGUIER, *Aristandre et Cléonice*, p. 5 f.

[33] It appears that the comment on Aristandre's attitude after his Rape of the Lock is intended to be satirical: "...jamais le fameux Jason ne fust si glorieux apres la conqueste de la toison d'or" (*ibid.*, p. 85).

EVOLUTION OF FORM AND STYLE 113

Another stylistic tendency which may be noted in all five novels is a turning away from oratorical monologues and stilted conversations cast in the form of dramatic dialogue.[34] In keeping with d'Audiguier's increased directness of expression, monologues and conversations are less frequently reproduced and usually show a greater degree of realism whenever they are quoted. Lysandre's lengthy speeches, for example, are restrained and straightforward in comparison with those of Lydamant—or, more vividly still, with that of the *châtelain*'s humiliated daughter, cited earlier.[35] The conversations recorded in *Les Diverses Affections* are generally terse and matter-of-fact. However, stylistic retrogression in *Aristandre et Cléonice* occurs in this respect also, for the ending of its final interpolated story is delayed by fourteen pages of monologues, of which Tiribase's six-page farewell address is of consummate tedium. In general, rhetorical eloquence tends to be more and more reserved for letters, which constitute a more suitable vehicle for it. But even though d'Audiguier stops using the sort of oratory delivered by the ex-soldier Tyrtée in *La Flavie* (in which four consecutive sentences beginning with "Aujourd'hui que" are followed by three beginning with "Allés"),[36] he never altogether abandons his irritating way of beginning each of a series of sentences with "Que" when narrating speeches and letters indirectly.

Instances of interpolated verse —probably no worse than that of any other minor poet of the day— occur several times in *Lysandre et Caliste* but only once in *Les Diverses Affections*. There is none in *Aristandre et Cléonice*, despite the seemingly favorable conditions of its plot for the inclusion of gallant verse.[37]

D'Audiguier's increasing directness is also reflected in his use of vivid but precise figures of speech instead of his earlier conven-

---

[34] In *La Flavie*, the young shepherd Pallante laments his pastoral isolation in language which d'Audiguier never again puts in the mouth of any character: "O nature fautiere, tu m'as iniquement germé d'un tyge boscager et sauvage, tu me devois anter sur une plante plus genereuse, dont les rameaux espandus et eslevés jusqu'au Ciel, fussent recognus et saluez de toute la terre; j'eusse faict paroistre qu'indignement tu m'as faict naistre dans un village, et mes exploits glorieux eussent retenti par tout l'Univers" (p. 8).

[35] See Chapter III.

[36] AUDIGUIER, *La Flavie*, p. 116.

[37] The popular vogue for embellishments of this sort had waned greatly by the 1620's. See REYNIER, *Le Roman sentimental*, p. 316 f.

tional expressions. There is a foretaste of this in *La Flavie*, when the Princess' apparently triumphant seducer prepares to dismount at the spot he has chosen "pour coucher les articles de leur accord". [38] Phylémon's malicious rumor about Callyante's attitude toward a less favored suitor is reported with rather appalling candor:

> Qu'il en pouvoit bien de loin adorer les fueilles, mais non pas en cueillir le fruit, le mener en main tous les jours, mais non pas la monter jamais. [39]

This tendency is particularly evident in his last two novels. Describing the childhood marriage of Minerve and her first husband, d'Audiguier remarks, "Come l'un ny l'autre n'estoyent capables d'amour, ils ne produisirent que de la haine". [40] When Tatius sells his magistracy, Minerve's relatives consider him "hors de ses estats, comme une pierre hors d'oeuvre". [41] The secrecy of this second marriage is promptly destroyed after its consummation, for "le ventre descouvrit peu de temps apres tout le mistere". [42] Legal separation from Tatius leaves Minerve with "ceste espine hors du pied". [43] When she is importuned by three suitors seeking to take her hand while walking in the Tuileries gardens, she remarks that she is old enough to be able to walk all by herself. Although not at fault in an argument with Minerve, Adraste is nevertheless obliged to apologize to her, "et le batu paya l'amende". [44] The sensual Minerve unwisely submits to her estranged husband's caresses, for she is neither "de bois, ny de marbre". [45] In amorous debates, she imitates cardsharps, "qui pour gagner tout l'argent d'autruy, perdent volontairement une partie de leur". [46]

---

[38] AUDIGUIER, *La Flavie*, p. 84.
[39] AUDIGUIER, *Lydamant et Callyante*, p. 52 A.
[40] AUDIGUIER, *Les Diverses Affections*, p. 4 A.
[41] *Ibid.*, p. 34 A.
[42] *Ibid.*, p. 30 A.
[43] *Ibid.*, p. 38 A.
[44] *Ibid.*, p. 67 A.
[45] *Ibid.*, p. 127 B. Cf. AUDIGUIER, *Lysandre et Caliste*, p. 26; Caliste is first touched by Lysandre's declarations of love for the same reason.
[46] AUDIGUIER, *Les Diverses Affections*, p. 99 A.

Similar examples occur throughout *Aristandre et Cléonice*. Queen Albanie quickly realizes that her storyteller Arsilée has "quelque dent de lait contre Cléonice". [47] When Cléonice discovers that Aristandre has surreptitiously acquired a lock of her hair, "il ne faloit point de lunettes pour voir qu'elle estoit faschée". [48] During the crossroads fight with Polinic in the "Marriage to a Statue" story, Icar seizes his enemy, "qui se laisse manier comme un baston". [49] Aristandre's accomplice gives Cléonice's mother a singularly blunt warning about an imaginary rumor said to be circulating at Court:

> on dit que Mademoiselle vostre fille est grosse, et que vous l'en emmenez afin qu'elle n'accouche point icy à la veuë de la Cour. [50]

Arsilée moves quickly to take advantage of Cléonice's illness, "prenant ceste occasion aux cheveux". [51] When further opportunity for mischief presents itself, she "faisoit deux coups d'une mesme pierre". [52] Threatened with reprisal, she becomes cautious, "oyant toucher ceste grosse corde". [53] But she is always resourceful, having "plusieurs cordes en son arc". [54]

The final interpolated story of the novel, that of Tiribase the gentleman pirate, provides two more instances of this direct, candid expression. Down on his luck, Tiribase is described as being "si accoquiné à sa misere, qu'il n'eut point honte de la produire". [55] As the final significant figure in d'Audiguier's last novel, he is far removed from the lofty (and wholly conventional) idealism of Francus and even from the Petrarchan conflict of Lydamant in

---

[47] AUDIGUIER, *Aristandre et Cléonice*, p. 71.
[48] *Ibid.*, p. 88. Cf. AUDIGUIER, *Lydamant et Callyante*, p. 134 A, where the same figure is used to describe Callyante's wrathful appearance.
[49] AUDIGUIER, *Aristandre et Cléonice*, p. 151.
[50] *Ibid.*, p. 259.
[51] *Ibid.*, p. 205.
[52] *Ibid.*, p. 208.
[53] *Ibid.*, p. 159. Cf. AUDIGUIER, *Lysandre et Caliste*, p. 349; despite the intimacy forced upon Lysandre and Caliste in fleeing to Brussels, he hesitates to assail her virtue again: "...il n'osa point encore toucher ceste corde."
[54] AUDIGUIER, *Aristandre et Cléonice*, p. 209.
[55] *Ibid.*, p. 334.

his passion for Callyante. Tiribase is noble but improvident and will resort to piracy and fraud to achieve his goals. He loves Orithie, but his motivation for this is unlike that of any previous d'Audiguier hero: "...et pour ses richesses, et pour sa beauté". [56] With this depressingly realistic note, d'Audiguier's general evolution from stylized, saccharine expresion to bluntly candid observation reaches its ultimate development.

---

[56] *Ibid.*, p. 312.

Chapter VII

THE PUBLISHING HISTORY OF *LYSANDRE ET CALISTE*

D'Audiguier's most successful work, *Lysandre et Caliste*, seems to have had a power of entertainment which maintained a degree of popularity for it long after his other novels had been forgotten. Alone of all his works, this story was recast as a play by Pierre Du Ryer (Hardy's youthful foe) in a tragi-comedy entitled *Lisandre et Caliste*. This tragi-comedy was performed at the Hôtel de Bourgogne in 1603 and was published in 1632.[1] The novel itself enjoyed a publishing history which deserves special attention both for the multiplicity of its editions and for the shift in popular fictional taste which is reflected in them.

Of the fifty-one known editions of this novel in various forms,[2] twenty were reprints of the original 1615 edition, published during the following ninety-two years in Paris, Lyon, Rouen, Amsterdam, and Brussels.[3] In addition, one French-German and four French-Dutch bilingual editions were published in Leyden and Amsterdam between 1650 and 1670.

---

[1] Paris: Pierre David. Although the novel has ten books, Du Ryer's tragi-comedy is based only on the last five, beginning with Lysandre's duel with Cloridan. The role of the Parisian butcher was played at the Hôtel de Bourgogne by Gros Guillaume. See LANCASTER, p. 316; see also H. C. LANCASTER, *A History of French Dramatic Literature in the Seventeenth Century. Part I: The Pre-Classical Period (1610-1634)* (Baltimore and Paris: Johns Hopkins Press and Presses Universitaires de France, 1929), II, 484.

[2] See Appendix B for a consolidated bibliography of these editions.

[3] It may be recalled that *L'Astrée* was never reprinted again from 1647 until well into our own century and appeared in only five abridgements or reworkings during the same period. See O.-C. REURE, "La Vie et les œuvres de Honoré d'Urfé" (Paris: Librairie Plon, 1910), p. 214.

Translations of the novel were published in four languages, also with a total of twenty editions.[4] Four editions of an English translation were printed in London between 1621 and 1652. In Amsterdam, there appeared four editions in Dutch alone between 1632 and 1703, in addition to the bilingual editions mentioned earlier. Four editions of a German translation were published in the Netherlands between 1644 and 1670. There were also two editions of an Italian translation, published in 1663 and 1671.

In view of d'Audiguier's own theory of brazenly inventive translation, noted earlier, it is interesting to observe the effort exerted to adapt this conventional French adventure novel to foreign tastes. Th otherwise dutiful English translation omits the Mont Valérien hermitage episode, thereby hastening the inevitable marriage of Lysandre and Caliste and promptly terminating the novel with some remaining momentum; this tidy English conclusion also dispenses with the highly distracting supernatural events at the wedding banquet as well as d'Audiguier's unseemly description of the wedding night enjoyed by five couples. Forty years later, Maiolino Bisaccioni undertook to translate the work into Italian as accurately as possible while rectifying the peculiarities and excesses of the original. Although reworking rather than translating the last section of the novel, Bisaccioni usually remained faithful to d'Audiguier's text. Yet he made a number of arbitrary suppressions and modifications which Procacci attributes to the translator's personal concern for restraint and propriety during this period of his career.[5] Such questionable details as the slaughter of birds in flight by the shout of a crowd below or Lysandre's marvelous disgorging of penknives, images, cartnails, and the like are typical omissions. According to Procacci, Bisaccioni almost invariably sought to reduce that which seemed excessively long-winded or artificial to more modest and natural proportions. Unfortunately, his version leaves much to be desired in its expression, having obviously been hurriedly composed.[6] It is not hard to

---

[4] Here again, it may be noted that complete and partial translations of *L'Astrée* were limited to ten editions during the same period (*ibid.*, p. 222).

[5] PROCACCI, p. 229.

[6] *Ibid.*, p. 230.

imagine the compounded effect of such a version based on a hasty, carelessly composed original.

In 1735, there appeared a reworking of the novel by Guillot de la Chassagne entitled *Le Chevalier des Essars, et la comtesse de Berci*. While retaining most of d'Audiguier's basic plot and many of his fictional devices, the revisor substituted conventional French names for the original pseudo-Classical nomenclature and made substantial modifications in the language and behavior of the characters as part of his effort to modernize the novel for contemporary readers. His success may be judged from the publication of seven editions of this revision in 1735 alone, with an eighth edition appearing in 1750. In acknowledging his source, Guillot de la Chassagne is without gratitude, not even deigning to name d'Audiguier as the original author:

> Au reste la lecture du Manuscrit où je les [les faits] ai recueillis m'a coûté beaucoup de peine et d'ennui. Sans parler du langage peu intelligible de cet Ecrit, j'y ai trouvé presque par-tout un style enflé et peu naturel, des comparaisons fréquentes et outrées, et sur-tout une morale extrêmement fatiguante. Mais j'ai cru devoir faire grace au goût et au langage des siècles passez en faveur d'un grand nombre d'évenements singuliers et interessans dont cette Histoire est remplie.[7]

In 1785, an anonymous editor's condensation of the original version of the novel was published in the *Bibliothèque universelle des romans*. The first seven "books" of this eighty-two page version of a novel originally nearly eight hundred pages long do reproduce the essence of the corresponding divisions of the original, although with notable modifications of language and detail. However, the editor abruptly compresses the 190 pages of Books VIII and IX into a six-page section which purports to show the remarkable ability of the author "pour prolonger les embarras, et forcer son Lecteur, pour ainsi dire, le pistolet sur la gorge".[8] As a result, only the barest summary of indispensable events survives of d'Audi-

---

[7] [ABBÉ IGNACE VINCENT GUILLOT DE LA CHASSAGNE], *Le Chevalier des Essars, et la comtesse de Berci* (Amsterdam: Wetstein et Smith, 1735), I, xvf.

[8] *Bibliothèque universelle*, p. 76.

guier's web of adventures and coincidences. Likewise, when the 165 pages of Book X are reduced to eight, many of its reversals are abandoned without apology, not an altogether blameworthy deed in view of d'Audiguier's interminably dilatory procedure in that final chapter.

The last known version of this novel, published in the *Nouvelle Bibliothèque des Romans* in 1799, is actually a condensation of Guillot de la Chassagne's revision of 1735. Surprisingly enough, this second-hand condensation adheres somewhat more closely to the original plot than does the direct condensation of 1785, despite the even greater brevity made necessary by its mere seventy pages. Its tone is of course more modern, abetted in this by French nomenclature as well as Classical refinement and restraint of speech and sentiment far removed from the outlook and experience of d'Audiguier (and most of his original readers).

These two final versions of *Lysandre et Caliste* have a particular interest, for they reflect the changed opinion of what constituted commercially acceptable fiction nearly two hundred years after the first edition, with the advent, reign, and decadence of French Classicism occurring in the interval. The fact that these are condensations is important in view of the editors' obligation to determine which details were most worthy of retention after establishing the basic plot.

As was pointed out earlier, the 1785 direct condensation does preserve most of the substance of d'Audiguier's plot. However, an examination of the original quickly reveals a number of important changes and omissions in its presentation. To begin with, the sexual compatibility of Cléandre and Caliste now receives considerably less emphasis, being described in one restrained sentence. There is no longer any psychological analysis of Béronte, Cléandre's jealous brother, who is described as "un peu jaloux [de Lysandre] sans savoir pourquoi". [9] During Lysandre's clandestine rendezvous with Caliste, the condensed version seeks to augment the suspense of Cléandre's unexpected call and Lysandre's later headlong flight while bowdlerizing the vigorous seduction attempt. But in this

---

[9] *Ibid.*, p. 13.

same episode, the symbolic dragon of Cléandre's alarming dream is no longer mentioned.

Very little is said about the Holland campaign, and the site of the returning knights' public combat is transferred from the Arsenal square to the Place Royale (not yet constructed in the original). Lysandre's song about Ypolite is no longer coincidental but is represented as having been written for the later would-be mistress, identified here as his former Gascon sweetheart. There is no miraculous cure after his ambush, although the despairing physicians "gardèrent un funeste silence" [10] at first. Only a restrained description is given of his disappointment at the rejection of his second seduction attempt. The remarkable supernatural aspects of his illness are omitted, as is most of the pious scene with Clairange.

The long scene of the pilgrim Lysandre's reunion with Cléandre and Lydian at Montserrat is reduced to a quick summary, while the editor omits their subsequent call on Clairange at his monastery and Lydian's sacrilegious appeal to his mistress Olinde upon returning to Paris. Gone is the unpleasantly vivid detail of Lysandre's medical indisposition at the time of Cloridan's challenge, and the aftermath of the duel itself is greatly abridged. The "Grateful Ghost" motif is totally suppressed, as are all but a few lines of Cléandre's dying farewell. Although Caliste's grief in prison is not referred to, the editor attributes lamentation "indigne d'un Cavalier" [11] to Lysandre in Flanders.

Among several minor changes in the circumstances of Caliste's escape, no mention is made of the presence of the executioner and the prison clerk at the warden's Twelfth Night party; at the same time, suspense is heightened by an interpolated description of the guard's fumbling with the wrong key while trying to deliver Caliste to her rescuers. All details of the flight to Brussels and Frisia are omitted, including the account of Lysandre's rekindled passion and Caliste's promise of marriage after their ultimate vindication. After their return to France, Lydian is represented as becoming angry upon learning of the alleged Lysandre-Ypolite affair, which he —and not his father Dorilas— reports indignantly to Caliste.

---

[10] *Ibid.*, p. 35.
[11] *Ibid.*, p. 65.

An important suppression is that of the combat between the disguised Ypolite and Lysandre's enemy Lucidan; her coming to Paris —weakly motivated— now leads to a chance encounter with Caliste while both are wandering through the countryside. Also eliminated with this combat is the second royal pardon, granted upon Béronte's timely intercession in the original. No details are given about the London tourney, its remarkable prizes, or the French knights' participation.

Lucidan is represented as falling in love with Caliste upon her return from Longchamps, although in the original he had transferred his affections to Ypolite by this time. Instead of donning Caliste's armor, Ypolite now disguises herself in Lydian's "chapeau militaire et les autres habillemens". [12] After wounding and abandoning her, Lysandre is not only urged to return by her valet (no longer an equally Amazonian *suivante*) but also by Clairange. However, there is no longer any pressing need to reach Paris, for the great combat between Lysandre's father and Cléandre's vindictive kinsman Varasque is omitted. Ypolite and Lysandre arrive to find themselves already fully vindicated by Léon's confession.

A major departure from the original plot occurs when Ypolite generously resolves to end all hatred and jealousy —and to restore Caliste's compromised honor— by offering her hand to Lucidan, who is described as already "piqué de l'inconséquence de Caliste". [13] The dilatory Mont Valérien hermitage episode is eliminated, and the condensation is promptly terminated with a wedding unmarked by preliminary contest or later supernatural apparitions and without the erotic transports which originally ended the novel.

From a linguistic standpoint, a conscious effort at modernization may be observed. Attempting to reconcile Clairange and Lydian before their duel in Book I, Lysandre originally said, "Bon-jour, Messieurs, quel differend avez-vous? que je vous accorde". [14] This candid, unpolished address now assumes a more discreet and somewhat unctuous form: "Il me semble, Messieurs, que vous avez besoin d'un tiers pour vous accorder". [15] Another instance is the

---

[12] *Ibid.*, p. 84.
[13] *Ibid.*, p. 89.
[14] AUDIGUIER, *Lysandre et Caliste*, p. 47.
[15] *Bibliothèque universelle*, p. 17.

replacement of Lysandre's archaic protestation, "Nenny, Nenny",[16] by the modern and flatly conventional "Non, Monsieur, non".[17] D'Audiguier's disdainful reference to the Parisian rabble as "le levrier ordinaire du bourreau"[18] becomes less vivid as "le lévrier ordinaire des chasseurs d'hommes".[19] The evil Clarinde is no longer rehired by "la trop facile et pitoyable Caliste"[20] but rather by "cette belle et vertueuse Dame".[21] The editor even sees fit to enhance the local color of d'Audiguier's Parisian setting by referring to the unidentified church at the beginning of Book VI as St-Paul, demolished in the Revolution six years after the condensation appeared.

The 1799 condensation of Guillot de la Chassagne's reworking tends to omit fewer elements of the original plot but at the same time often modifies or supplements it at will. At the very outset, Caliste is no longer represented as Cléandre's thoroughly satisfied mate but instead as a less formidable Princesse de Clèves, with friendship and esteem but not sensual love for her husband, whom she has married as a filial duty. Only Lysandre is able to win that love, which she firmly keeps within the bounds of propriety with greater assurance than in the original, for she is now represented as "aussi sage que belle",[22] and her conduct is no less pure than her love. Lysandre, too, appears to have a thicker veneer of civilization than before, no longer giving way to brutal rage and violent recrimination when his improper advances are spurned; gentlemanly declarations of respect and fidelity consistently replace his original ranting. The perfidious Clarinde, who gradually fell prey to debauchery in d'Audiguier's account because of moral instability, is now damned from the outset as having been "née avec tous les vices".[23]

Cléandre's interruption of Lysandre' bedroom rendezvous with Caliste is made even more trying by the protraction of the amorous

---

[16] AUDIGUIER, *Lysandre et Caliste*, p. 253.
[17] *Bibliothèque universelle*, p. 57.
[18] AUDIGUIER, *Lysandre et Caliste*, p. 310.
[19] *Bibliothèque universelle*, p. 70.
[20] AUDIGUIER, *Lysandre et Caliste*, p. 226.
[21] *Bibliothèque universelle*, p. 50.
[22] *Nouvelle Bibliothèque*, p. 59.
[23] *Ibid.*, p. 70.

husband's visit in her bed. The dragon motif of Cléandre's dream is omitted as in the 1785 condensation. Lysandre's ensuing seduction attempt —obliquely mentioned— is stopped by Caliste with an outraged but improbably eloquent speech delivered from a supine position.

After little deviation from the original plot for several episodes, the editor interpolates an affectionate farewell interview between Lysandre and Caliste just before the Holland expedition; coming upon them unexpectedly, Béronte suspects the nature of their meeting. During the expedition, Caliste visits her parents in Burgundy rather than Normandy. Her friend Olinde is now openly labelled a coquette for her treatment of Clairange and Lydian. After returning to Paris, Lysandre entertains his friends with lute-accompanied songs, the significance of which only Béronte —not Caliste— is able to grasp. When Lysandre is ambushed, physicians fear him to be mortally wounded. "Heureusement la faculté ne juge pas en dernier ressort",[24] and he recovers without benefit of the original miraculous cure. Instead of riding off in a rage against Caliste when rebuffed for the second time, Lysandre remains in Paris to serve her dutifully.

But at this point, the editor inserts Lysandre's mortal combat with Cloridan, who is represented as having been directly responsible for the ambush. Instead of fleeing to Brussels to escape persecution, Lysandre takes refuge at Cléandre's estate in Anjou. Meanwhile, Clairange turns to the religious life but becomes a Knight of Malta rather than a Capuchin.

Although the "Grateful Ghost" episode is eliminated from the account of Cléandre's trip to Italy, now in Lydian's company, the trip is greatly altered in that the two are successfully carried to Oran by their pirate captor and are ultimately ransomed through the good offices of Lysandre. The ensuing reunion in Paris marks Guillot de la Chassagne's return to d'Audiguier's narration after omitting the Montserrat episode.

The circumstances of Cléandre's murder are substantially altered, for it occurs at his Paris town house when Léon is trapped there by Cléandre's early return home with Caliste from a ball. In this

---

[24] *Ibid.*, p. 87.

version, Lysandre is present as his dying friend urges Caliste to love Lysandre with the same tenderness he himself has enjoyed; no mention is made of Lysandre's sword, a prominent detail in the original.

Another change is seen in Caliste' deliberate choice to prove her innocence legally against Clarinde's charge instead of fleeing at once with Lysandre, whom she orders to escape. The circumstances of her own escape from the Petit Châtelet—although greatly abridged—are basically those of the original, as are those of the flight to Brussels and Frisia. Unlike the original, Dorilas orders Caliste to return home to comfort her mother. Lysandre now takes refuge with an uncle in Gascony rather than with his parents.

The original plot is followed for Lysandre' conditional pardon, his relationship with Ypolite, and his impromptu trip to London for the great tourney. Few details about this event are given, apart from the amazing prizes awarded him. Rejoicing in victory with his friends, whose simultaneous presence in England is not adequately explained, Lysandre encounters and secures the cooperation of the penitent Léon at an English inn rather than during the shipwreck on Jersey of the original. The public combat between Lucidan and the disguised Ypolite is now terminated sooner with the vindication of Lysandre in regard to the death of Cloridan. Dismayed by her apparent rival's advent, Caliste flees to a convent in Etampes rather than to Longchamps. After the restoration of her honor, she persists in her belief that Lysandre has been unfaithful, an idea not in the original. To d'Audiguier's description of Lysandre's self-imposed exile at Mont Valérien, a sonnet not found in the original is added, with the unexpected editorial remark that it is high time for modern poets to cease imitating Racine and Boileau. After Béronte —not Lucidan— wins Ypolite's hand, the novel is concluded as in the original except for the omission of the supernatural events at the wedding banquet and d'Audiguier's description of the wedding night.[25] This last is instead replaced by a more edifying conclusion:

---

[25] Although a "nymph" does appear at this point in Guillot de la Chassagne's 1735 reworking, she is no longer a supernatural apparition but merely a beautiful young woman in costume who enters and pours out exquisite perfumes from her vase as a festive gesture (II, 428 f.).

> Unis par l'estime, les deux époux jouirent constamment d'un bonheur que n'altèrent ni les retours ni les changemens qui deshonorent presque tous les mariages, et le chevalier [Lysandre] eut de la comtesse [Caliste] des enfants qui héritèrent de leurs vertus. [26]

Guillot de la Chassagne's determination to renovate d'Audiguier's language to suit eighteenth-century tastes is apparent in his consistent substitution of new poems for those of the original, although these are certainly no more inspired than the earlier verse. The anonymous letter received by Lysandre after his ill-advised forest soliloquy is considerably more forceful and menacing than that of the original version. This increased loftiness of tone is also conspicuous in Caliste's longer speeches, which in their way are models of self-conscious eloquence if not of verisimilitude. For that matter, Lysandre expresses himself with a sustained refinement more typical of an eighteenth-century salon habitué than of a bellicose Gascon created in the image of Henri IV.

By examining both condensations, it is possible to establish in a general way not only what was of permanent fictional interest in d'Audiguier's novel but also those elements which had become wholly unacceptable or in need of modification for the general reading public —the novel-digest reading public— of the late eighteenth century. For the sake of convenience, these manifestations may be grouped in three categories.

The ageless nature of the love-triangle is again confirmed in this novel, as is an abiding fascination in the plight of a secret lover hidden in a bedroom while a husband makes love to his wife. Murder, ambush, and jailbreak continue to provide exciting entertainment. Resistance to parental matchmaking (despite the attractiveness of the lady proposed) remains topical, as does the problem of legal vindication in the face of unfavorable circumstantial evidence. Such ancient and threadbare fictional devices as mistaken identity and the overheard soliloquy can apparently still be used to advantage. Finally, the technique of ending a novel with a wedding (together with the suggestion of untroubled bliss there-

---

[26] *Nouvelle Bibliothèque*, p. 125.

after) is proved to be just as conventional in 1799 as it was in 1615, in the Byzantine romance, or in the Book of Ruth, for that matter.

On the other hand, artless eroticism is frowned upon in an age of elegant pornography, for both condensations omit d'Audiguier's enthusiastic wedding-night description. Likewise, unvarnished nationalism is no longer acceptable, as can be seen in the omission of every expression of fulsome royalist adulation as well as every anti-Spanish jibe of the Montserrat episode. This is also true of regional chauvinism, for d'Audiguier's scornful observations about Parisians, Normans, and Flemings have been eliminated. In good French Classical tradition, everything smacking of the supernatural has been cut out. No mention is made of a symbolic dragon in the report of Cléandre's dream. Lysandre's seemingly mortal wounds now are healed without recourse to a magician "opérateur". His later illness no longer involves vomiting unlikely objects which then become Capuchin relics. The "Grateful Ghost" motif is wholly dispensed with, and Cléandre now meets death without supernatural warning.[27] Perhaps most conspicuous of all is the elimination of nymph, storm, and prophetic obelisk during the final wedding banquet, a stylistically prudent omission made as early as 1627 in the English translation.

Among the elements requiring modification were d'Audiguier's attempts at eloquence. Whereas the language and style of lengthy speeches and letters now assume a modernized and over-polished form if they are retained, the original poetry is replaced by conventional verse of a more recent period. Gone are the frequent omniscient-author coments on the behavior of his characters, a device which did much to limit suspense in the original version. Related to these and also wholly eliminated are the author's own apostrophes, addressed with equal fervor to a character like Caliste or to such an entity as Fortune.

The complex relationships arising from the friendship of five couples and their relatives in the original version are greatly simplified in both condensations to focus more attention on the protagonists. The conventional chivalric atmosphere still acceptable in

---

[27] The ghost's visits were also eliminated in Du Ryer's play (1630). Cléandre's murder near the end of Act I occurs without any premonition of imminent death.

1615 is now transformed into that of a refined society of courtiers and their ladies. Although these courtiers are skilled in the use of weapons, the anachronism of armor is supplanted by contemporary military dress. D'Audiguier's emphasis on jousting as normal entertainment is greatly reduced, as is his portrayal of trial by combat, an outrageously anachronistic detail even in his own day. Tournaments and duels are still included but perfunctorily described. Religious elements are now sharply curtailed; gone are the lengthy sermons, exhortations, and pious reflections on death and the hereafter; gone are the disquieting aspects of the Montserrat episode, in which religious fervor, chauvinism, and comedy had been interwoven.

D'Audiguier's expansive insistence on the sexual compatibility of Cléandre and Caliste was evidently too forthright for later tastes, and their union is described with restraint. Perhaps sensing a lack of verisimilitude in a triangle where such an untroubled marriage exists, the eighteenth century seems to have preferred a "Princesse de Clèves" situation as being more understandable. Lysandre's behavior toward Caliste is considerably more dignified despite his carnal passion; instead of rages of frustration, his conduct is now marked by deference and patience.

Another notable change is the reading of moral lessons into the novel, which —even if implicit— were unimportant to d'Audiguier. On the contrary, the morality-conscious eighteenth century could savor the novel from standpoints to which the generation of Henri IV seems to have been generally indifferent. In both condensations, the public's attention is helpfully directed by editorial notes to these lessons as well as to useful comparisons revealing modern social blemishes and shortcomings. The 1799 version is even labelled "Quatrième Classe: Romans de Morale".[28]

The editors of both condensations express a number of personal opinions indicating their own attitude toward the novel. Aware of an inevitable gap between the spirit as well as the events of d'Audiguier's work and the experience of readers in the late eighteenth century, they strive to capitalize on a nostalgic admiration for a pleasantly remote past. In the 1785 version, after

---

[28] *Nouvelle Bibliothèque*, p. 58.

reproducing an abridged form of Clairange's first conversation with Lysandre, the editor notes,

> Tout ce que nous pourrons encore citer servira, non seulement à faire connoître le style, mais les mœurs, deux choses inséparables. Qu'on compare le discours de Clairange avec celui d'un Cavalier de nos jours qui seroit brouillé avec un autre.[29]

In the same vein, the editor dispatches the final scene of wedding festivities with a single bland statement reminiscent of the sort of literary expediency in which d'Audiguier himself indulged: "Il se fit de très belles fêtes, dont nous voudrions bien opposer la description à nos fêtes modernes".[30] D'Audiguier is not without honor as a novelist despite this *parvum ex multo* transformation of his work. After describing in some detail Lysandre's scheme to communicate with the imprisoned Caliste, the editor observes enthusiastically,

> On ne peut s'empêcher de faire observer à chaque pas le nœud de cette intrigue. On défie qu'il y ait un tort théâtral pour aucun des personnages.[31]

At another point, he comments,

> nos Romanciers modernes intriguent si peu, la délaient tant, parlent tant, qu'il ne seroit pas mal à propos de leur offrir des modèles, même de complication.[32]

But it is not to be forgotten that d'Audiguier lived and wrote before the dawn of French Classicism, as the editor indirectly reminds his readers:

> Nous le répétons, il y a certes du mérite à avoir fait cet Ouvrage dans l'enfance de l'art du Romancier; et tout Lecteur qui ne sera pas exclusivement épris de son siècle, trouvera du plaisir à lire cet Ouvrage.[33]

---

[29] *Bibliothèque universelle*, p. 16.
[30] *Ibid.*, p. 89.
[31] *Ibid.*, p. 7.
[32] *Ibid.*, p. 64.
[33] *Ibid.*, p. 76 f.

The editor of the 1799 version sees —or claims to see— a moral utility in its representation of noble love in another age, a love so different from the modern sort that this example is valuable even as proof that it once existed. The account of Cléandre's death provides an opportunity to reprove Revolutionary skepticism:

> Nos agréables trouveront cette mort bien religieuse; mais alors on croyoit au Dieu de ses Pères, et pourtant on avoit autant de vertu que de bravoure. [34]

D'Audiguier's condemnation of duelling enables the editor to decry the ferocious ascendancy of the seventeenth-century point of honor. More topical is the peril seen in the wicked Clarinde:

> Jeunes femmes qui lisez cette histoire, que la situation de la comtesse vous apprenne à examiner de près celles que le sort attache à votre service! Combien de ces filles ont perdu d'épouses qui, sans elles, n'auroient jamais oublié leurs devoirs. [35]

Finally, the editor declares the novel to be infinitely superior to the monstrous productions of modern novelists who have replaced God with a swarm of demons which encourage all manner of licentiousness. Conscious of the unclassical diffusion of d'Audiguier's plot, he defends it in terms which go far to explain the survival of the novel for 184 years:

> Il règne dans tout le cours de cette histoire un fond d'intérêt auquel il est impossible de se refuser. Peut-être en trouvera-t-on les incidents trop multipliés, mais on ne pourra disconvenir qu'ils sont amenés et conduits de manière à ce qu'aucun d'eux ne paroît invraisemblable. S'il en est qui semblent douteux, n'en accusons que le tems... [36]

---

[34] *Nouvelle Bibliothèque*, p. 103.
[35] *Ibid.*, p. 75.
[36] *Ibid.*, p. 125.

CHAPTER VIII

D'AUDIGUIER'S PERMANENT LITERARY SIGNIFICANCE

In view of d'Audiguier's later obscurity, the critical esteem in which he was held up to the time of the Académie Française dictionary project of 1638 is a curious situation. His intellectual and stylistic shortcomings have been noted, but the fact remains that he was considered to be a popular and entertaining writer during his lifetime, an opinion reflected in the attitude of the conservative Academicians even after the age of Gomberville and the *grands romans* had begun.

A clue to the reason for this popularity may be seen in the seemingly unjustified success of his incompetent translation of six *Novelas exemplares*. Despite frequent mistranslations of terms and reversals of inverted sentences as well as continual reliance on paraphrasing to circumvent apparently unfamiliar words and expressions in the original, these stories caught the fancy of the reading public much more than de Rosset's scrupulously faithful version of the other six.[1] In addition to the more conventional plots of d'Audiguier's series, however, this success appears to have been due in part to the vivid language and figures with which he compensated for his deficiencies as a linguist in reproducing Cervantes' prose. The necessity of paraphrasing allowed him to make use of an agile imagination in substituting material which would be entertaining to French readers unaware of a departure from the Spanish text.

---

[1] See Chapter II.

In his own fiction, d'Audiguier demonstrates an energetic, unshrinking eclecticism in assembling motifs from a wide range of literary sources. His criterion appears to have been the already proven or highly probable acceptability of such elements to a demanding but culturally deficient public made up largely of the Louvre-centered nobility of the day. As a member of that class, he imparts the masculine vigor of a proud though petty nobleman to each of his novels. None of them remains langorous for long, even *La Flavie* and *Lydamant et Callyante*, both written at the height of popular taste for the sentimental novel. The narration of adventures —both traditional and modern— is more natural to him than the comparatively static emotional rumination found in the works of many of his fellow novelists. Perhaps there is a special significance in those qualities of underlying realism and topical interest which became more and more apparent during his career. It may be that this characteristic feature of his writing aroused an unusual degree of empathy among his readers; for despite their taste for idealized portrayals of their own activities and surroundings, there can be little doubt that they were basically realistic in their outlook on life as well as being concerned with the immediacy of a tumultuous present. This type of self-identification in his fiction would provide a particular savor lacking in the works of equally conventional but less kindred spirits.

D'Audiguier's abrupt eclipse as an esteemed novelist seems to have occurred at approximately the same time as a cultural phenomenon arising from the prestige of social-literary salons like that of Madame de Rambouillet and was probably an immediate result of it. There is evidence that writers came to be recognized around 1630 as celebrities worth seeking after by virtue of their literary profession rather than as entertainers whose function in social gatherings corresponded in some ways to that of jesters during an earlier period:

> L'époque marque donc pour les écrivains une accession, une promotion sociale, qui facilitera, du point de vue moral, l'éclosion de nouvelles œuvres. Ils auront désormais un public, celui des "honnêtes gens" que Molière et les grands classiques reconnaîtront comme arbitres souverains du goût, s'étendant bien au delà de leurs confrères,

et susceptibles d'apprécier leurs ouvrages. Leur audience s'élargit et, fatalement, leur influence s'accroît.[2]

A new intellectualism came to shape the course of literature, which had previously tended to have its standards based on the unstable inclinations of a carelessly educated nobility. With the advent of favorable conditions for the establishment of at least theoretical standards for rule-abiding composition, the appearance of more even, elegant prose soon exposed by contrast the frequent negligence and artlessness of earlier writers. Once tolerated by an indulgent public, the works of authors like d'Audiguier came to be viewed unfavorably in comparison with the productions of more cautious literary artists.

The exaggeratedly affected language and ornamented style from which d'Audiguier had come close to breaking away was now virtually out of the question in fiction of the new generation. Novels of this period still included conversations, but the range of their content and variation was now greatly increased.[3] There were, of course, aspects of the new refined style which now seem just as patently artificial as the earlier attempts at eloquence in the novels of Nervèze and Des Escuteaux.[4] A dispassionate, oratorical quality came to pervade fiction, barring those unusual flashes of emotional realism which had enlivened d'Audiguier's novels despite their relatively unartistic bluntness.[5]

---

[2] GEORGES MONGRÉDIEN, *La Vie littéraire au XVIIe siècle* (Paris: J. Tallandier, 1947), p. 34.

[3] "A ce moment, la société mondaine a déjà fait son apprentissage... S'il est vrai que la galanterie reste le sujet préféré, on ne consentirait plus à en recevoir des leçons si directes, et, disons le mot, si puériles." (MAGENDIE, *Le Roman français au XVIIe siècle*, p. 317.)

[4] There is a strong tendency in modern critical opinion to make a sharp distinction between the "style Nervèze" of the first quarter of the century and the language and style of the *précieux* writers toward 1650, whereas scholars like Brunot and Mornet viewed the two as earlier and later manifestations of the same aspiration to refinement. See ADAM, "Baroque et Préciosité", *Revue des sciences humaines*, 1949 (nos. 53-56), 208-224. See also MONGRÉDIEN, p. 224 f.

[5] "On abandonne l'entassement des images, on recherche le vocabulaire correcte et juste, la phrase ample et bien équilibré, le développement logique et régulier; la solennité froide et académique s'installe dans le style; elle est aussi éloigné de la pratique ordinaire que l'usage incessante de la métaphore. Le caractère commun à beaucoup de grands romans... est que le

In a more general way, the period saw a dissemination of salon *politesse*—a sense of propriety in language and in the choice of topics considered to be suitable for discussion—to the French middle class from the relatively isolated coteries which flourished during the first quarter of the century. If the new artistic emphasis of the period required refinement of style, the broadening cult for social propriety was no less committed to a thorough-going refinement of literary expression, both in the author's selection of themes and in his vocabulary. The direct representation of physical passion and its successful or attempted gratification was firmly proscribed, as was any term which had an unpleasantly concrete meaning of a sexual nature.[6] This prohibition alone would have eliminated a great many of d'Audiguier's most vivid (and most realistic) episodes in all five of his novels. It would have required a restraint very foreign to his personality.

It has been observed that the artificiality of the sentimental novel arose partly from an ill-advised literary fusion in the early seventeenth century in which prose was often endowed with the linguistic equipment of poetry.[7] The inflated style which resulted from this tradition was doomed to quick obsolescence. D'Audiguier came close to freeing himself from such a moribund conception of prose after his first two novels. However, his style and language were often guilty of the opposite excess in the unadorned, pedestrian directness found in his later novels. At the time of his death, his continued popularity was already jeopardized by an apparent inability to break completely with the basically sixteenth-century tradition of the episodic adventure novel involving chivalric or pseudo-chivalric motifs. There is no way to determine how successfully he might have adapted his style and language to the standards of 1630 if he had survived into that age of intellectual refinement. In view of his advancing years at the time of

---

style parlé a l'air d'être du style écrit." (MAGENDIE, *Le Roman français du XVIIe siècle*, p. 345.)

[6] For example, Magendie indicates that the word "pucelage" had fallen into disfavor as early as 1626 (*ibid.*, p. 71). The *châtelain*'s daughter would have been obliged to use a more oblique reference to the treasure spurned by the disguised Statyre in *Lydamant et Callyante*.

[7] See BICHLMAIER, p. 82.

his murder, it appears unlikely that he could have made a major adjustment of this sort.

He was perhaps fortunate to have been spared the terrible humiliation which befell his contemporary Alexandre Hardy soon after d'Audiguier's murder. The young poets who assailed Hardy's reputation in 1628 were representatives of an impatient new generation which was revolting against the outmoded conceptions and techniques characteristic of the old dramatist's works.[8] The parallel between Hardy and d'Audiguier is quite striking; both authors wrote with an unpolished vigor which came not to be tolerated in an age of literary refinement and restraint. Proud as he was, d'Audiguier would surely have resented public ridicule for literary obsolescence as much as he had been offended by scorn for his indigence or his precarious social position.

The contemporary vogue and subsequent decline of d'Audiguier's literary reputation are matters of historical fact. Just what permanent judgment d'Audiguier earned as a novelist can only be a statement of relatively informed opinion. Remarkably varied in motif and characterization but uneven and negligent in its presentation, his prose fiction reveals him to have been an imaginative, versatile near-professional in this genre. His failure to produce a single artistic masterpiece of fiction may apparently be attributed to his own uneven cultural background as well as to the lack of intellectual and literary sophistication on the part of his reading public. The motivation which prompted him to write novels, translations, editions, and poetry probably hindered his artistic development further; his frequently expressed awareness of the important but unappreciated role of literature in society seems to have been overshadowed in practice by exigencies of time and money.

---

[8] "Du torrent de paroles et de la bordée d'injures à l'adresse de ses ennemis il résulte indubitablement que Hardy se rend compte qu'il est devancé par des dramaturges de la nouvelle école. Son langage, son style, sa technique sont hors d'usage. Tout en vivant au XVIIe siècle, il a continué à produire des œuvres qui rappellent le XVIe siècle. Hardy est demeuré stationnaire. Mais l'art dramatique poursuit son évolution, il ne connaît pas de longues périodes d'arrêt." (S. WILMA DEIERKAUF-HOLSBOER, "Vie d'Alexandre Hardy, poète du roi", *Proceedings of the American Philosophical Society*, XCI [1947], no. 4, 370.)

Yet d'Audiguier deserves more emphatic recognition than he has hitherto received for the multi-lingual publishing success of *Lysandre et Caliste,* whatever its artistic shortcomings. In composing that work, he became the unwitting provider of a valuable index to changing popular taste in fiction from the end of the Renaissance in France to the beginning of French Romanticism.

In addition to this claim to a certain deference, he has another, less obvious sort of interest for modern students of seventeenth-century French literature. This study has attempted to show that his novels are representative of French prose fiction written for the non-erudite reading public during the first quarter of the century. As reflections of his own active and tragic life, they are pervaded by a realistic energy and frustrated idealism of an unusually vivid sort. In this respect, d'Audiguier is entitled to a distinctive position among the lesser known novelists of the period, for his fiction successfully bridges the gap of years to reveal his own strangely sympathetic personality and that of the restless generation of transition to which he belonged.

APPENDIX A

PLOT SUMMARIES OF D'AUDIGUIER'S NOVELS

1. *La Flavie de la Menor*

>   FRANCUS, Hector's son, founder and ruler of France.
>   FILAMOR, Francus' follower and confidant.
>   MATHILDE, Queen Mother of Aquitania.
>   FLAVIE, Princess of Aquitania, Mathilde's daughter, Hercules' granddaughter.
>   BELYSARE, Prince of Aquitania, Flavie's brother.
>   PERSES, Prince of Albania, Mathilde's guest.
>   MARTAN, Prince of Spain, Flavie's cousin.
>   MERLAN, African knight and magician in Martan's retinue.
>   MARTHÉSIE, Amazon daughter of Hector and Penthesileia, Belysare's beloved.
>   PALLANTE, Marthésie's twin brother, raised as a shepherd.
>   TYRTÉE, former Trojan soldier, Pallante's shepherd guardian.

First Book. Having escaped death in the destruction of Troy, Hector's son Francus has made his way across Europe to Gaul, where he has established a kingdom named after himself, with a new Troy named after his uncle Paris for its capital. Meanwhile, Hercules' son Vasco, the ruler of Aquitania (hence, Gascony), has died after a glorious life, leaving his widow Mathilde, his son Belysare, and his daughter Flavie. Young Belysare decides to seek military glory and goes off to emulate his ancestors, leaving affairs of state to his mother.

Arriving in Thrace, he spends, a night with a group of shepherds, of whom the most striking is Pallante, a handsome youth of remarkably noble mien and bearing. Two wayfaring soldiers, also invited to spend the night, reveal themselves to be in the service of the warrior-maid Marthésie, now on her way to Gaul to help Princess Flavie in an impending war against Spain. Since Marthésie is Belysare's beloved, he eagerly learns of her winning a single combat that very day with a young Trojan knight, Filamor, who before dying had revealed the reason for his presence in Thrace. As Francus' follower and confidant, he had overcome his own secret passion for his master's beloved Flavie in accompanying Francus on a diplomatic mission to Mathilde's court in Belysare's absence. The arrival of Flavie's lustful and scheming young cousin, Prince Martan of Spain, had created an intolerable situation for Francus, who had withdrawn in hurt pride with Filamor. After their departure, Martan had decided to overcome Flavie's unrelenting resistance to his advances by kidnaping her with the magical help of his African follower Merlan, pretending to be rescuing her from unknown abductors. After Flavie had successfully resisted his attempts on her virtue, Martan carried her off toward Spain but was prevented from forcing her submission along the way by the timely coincidental arrival of Francus and Filamor, who overcame and killed him and all his restinue except Merlan. The joyful reunion of maiden and friends was interrupted by the return of Merlan and a squadron of ghosts, whose appearance caused the frightened horses to carry off their riders in different directions. Filamor had been seeking Francus across Europe at the time of his ill-fated combat with Marthésie.

Second Book. Belysare leaves at once to seek Marthésie. Pallante now learns from his old guardian Tyrtée that he is actually the son of Hector and Penthesileia, thus Francus' half-brother as well as Marthérie's twin. Convinced that the time has come for Pallante to attempt to avenge his family and refound Troy, the old guardian presents him with Hector's sword and two vases of money preserved for this occasion. Abandoning the pastoral life, Pallante leaves the next day to undertake this mission.

Third Book. Flavie has been saved from Merlan and the ghosts by a venerable old man who leads her through a grotto into a beautiful antipodal dale. She learns that it has been necessary to bring her here to inform her of her long-ordained destiny of marrying Francus and creating the most glorious posterity in history, the kings of France, shown to her as wall images. As she is admiring the most conspicuous of these, depicting Henri IV with Marie de Médicis, the revelation is cut off by thunder and lightning.

Meanwhile, Francus has extended his search for Flavie to the sea. As he approaches an island in the South Atlantic, he learns that it was the scene of a remarkable episode in which a vindictive king nearly had his own long-kidnaped son sacrificed with the boy's beloved before a last-minute recognition through coincidence. Upon landing, Francus is nearly slain by a monster but is saved by an unknown knight.

The scene shifts abruptly to Marthésie, now in Spain seeking Flavie. She encounters Merlan, engages and defeats him in combat, and slays him in pitiless wrath upon discovering his sword to be that of the murdered Prince Perses of Albania.

2. *Les Douces Affections de Lydamant et de Callyante*

> LYDAMANT, young French knight at Henri IV's court.
> CALLYANTE, young French noblewoman, Lydamant's beloved.
> THERMODON, Lydamant's rival for Callyante's hand.
> STATYRE, Lydamant's sister, trained as a knight.
> REGNIER, Venetian senator and Statyre's foster-father.
> PALÉMON, Callyante's kinsman and Lydamant's friend.
> PHYLÉMON, unsuccessful and slanderous suitor of Callyante.

First Book. Discouraged in his courtship of Callyante, the young knight Lydamant goes off to Hungary to fight in an expedition against the Turks. Callyante's compassion for him, rekindled by news of his prowess, turns to despair at the false report of his death. Finally resigned to her loss, she defers to her father's will in agreeing to marry Thermodon. Returning to Court, Lydamant is plunged in grief at learning what has happened and rides off aimlessly through the countryside. Stopping for the night at an inn, he is strangely attracted to another young knight, who reminds him vaguely of Callyante. The author reveals that the other knight is actually Lydamant's own sister Statyre, whom he has never seen and whose kinship is not known to him. She has been reared by the retired Venetian senator, former governor of Cyprus, and astrologer Regnier after the fatal miscarriage of her mother when told of the death of her husband while on her way to attempt to ransom him from Turkish captivity. Having received training in the use of weapons as part of her education, the beautiful Statyre has been dispatched in disguise by Regnier to deliver a message to the now-famous Lydamant, for whom Regnier knows she has a secret but innocent affection (not realizing her kinship).

Second Book. Next morning, Statyre delivers Regnier's letter to Lydamant, whose identity (but not kinship) she has guessed. Lydamant suspects that Regnier's invitation to come to his Venetian mainland estate may be a scheme to introduce him there to Statyre, of whose beauty Lydamant has heard. Nevertheless, he agrees to accompany the still unidentified messenger to Italy, while secretly resolving to remain faithful to Callyante. En route, Lydamant agrees to reveal the cause of his obvious sadness and tells of his first acquaintance with Callyante and his success in becoming her favorite suitor.

Third Book. Lydamant then tells of the downfall of his happiness, the result of a malicious rumor spread by an unsuccessful rival, Phylémon. Both Callyante and her father are offended by the taint of scandal, and the moody Lydamant worsens the situation in several painful interviews with her, which culminate in his decision to go off to Hungary.

Fourth Book. As their trip to Italy continues, the two companions are importuned one night in their beds by the daughters of their *châtelain* host. Lydamant cheerfully accepts his visitor's proposition but Statyre's necessary refusal humiliates and enrages the other girl, who sends her fiancé and his brother to punish these discourteous guests the following day. Maintaining her disguise, Statyre helps Lydamant defeat their challengers with dispatch. Finally arriving at Regnier's estate, brother and sister are mutually identified by Regnier, who further delights Lydamant with astrological assurances as to the ultimate success of his courtship. A few days later, Lydamant takes leave of Regnier and Statyre in order to return promptly to Callyante.

Fifth Book. While returning to France, Lydamant comes upon a bridge guarded by a knight in black armor and learns that every passing French knight must either leave his name and that of his beloved or else defeat the Black Knight in combat. Outraged at seeing the names of Phylémon and Callyante among the many displayed there, he assails the challenger and overcomes him in furious combat. He then learns that his defeated, wounded adversary is his old friend (and Callyante's kinsman) Palémon, who tells his still unidentified vainquisher of Callyante's efforts to find Lydamant after the sudden death of Thermodon and of her father. He then describes his own attempt to help her find Lydamant by establishing this check-point for passing French knights. That very morning he had forced the passing Phylémon to leave that tangible proof of his unworthiness. Lydamant now reveals his identity, and the reunited friends set out together to return to Callyante as quickly as possible.

Sixth Book. Sailing from Ostia in an effort to travel faster by sea, the two friends are blown off course and cast up on an unfamiliar island. A passerby escorts them to the nearby Isle Volante, inhabited entirely by thieves living in a wholly selfish and materialistic society with no respect for true social or literary merit. Continuing on their way, the two friends soon reach Callyante's estate only to be glacially received by her, for Phylémon had spread another false rumor, alleging Lydament's marriage to Statyre. Lydamant's sighs and tears finally melt Callyante to an equally tearful realization of her own ingratitude toward him. After an exchange of self-justifications, Callyante graciously admits defeat and consents to their prompt marriage, which takes place amid general rejoicing.

3. *Histoire trage-comique de nostre temps, sous les noms de Lysandre et de Caliste*

LYSANDRE, young French knight at Henri IV's court.
CALISTE, young French noblewoman, the object of Lysandre's illicit desire.
CLÉANDRE, husband of Caliste and friend of Lysandre.
DORILAS, Caliste's father.
ORONTE, Caliste's mother.
LYDIAN, Caliste's brother.
OLINDE, young noblewoman, beloved of Lydian.
CLAIRANGE, Lydian's rival.
ALCIDON, friend of Lydian.
ARGIRE, Alcidon's beloved.
VARASQUE, Cléandre's older kinsman.
BÉRONTE, Cléandre's brother.
AMBRISE, Lysandre's young widowed sister and Béronte's beloved.
CLARINDE, Caliste's attendant and betrayer.
LÉON, Béronte's friend, Clarinde's paramour, and Cléandre's murderer.

CLORIDAN, Lysandre's challenger in a duel fatal to himself.
CRISANTE, Cloridan's second, also fatally wounded.
LUCIDAN, Crisante's kinsman and later plaintiff against Lysandre.
YPOLITE, Amazonian noblewoman in love with Lysandre, later Lucidan's beloved.
BÉRANGER, Frisian admirer of Caliste, killed in self-defense by Lysandre.
HENRI IV.
MARIE DE MÉDICIS.

First Book. Of all his blessings, the illustrious young nobleman Cléandre is most fortunate in having as his wife one of the most beautiful women in France, Caliste. The fullness of their marriage seems ideal, but their bliss is jeopardized by the obsessive secret passion of the valiant young knight Lysandre. Abandoning his previous concern for military glory, he lays the groundwork for future advances by cultivating Cléandre's friendship, a tactic which earns him the friendly devotion of both husband and wife. Having been taken to their country estate (Beauplan) near Paris to recover from the wasting effects of his secret passion, Lysandre accidentally reveals his true feelings in an outdoor soliloquy overheard by Caliste and her brother-in-law Béronte, who is already jealous of Cléandre's affection for the newcomer. Receiving their anonymous letter urging his departure, Lysandre succeeds in diplomatically trapping Caliste into admitting her part in the letter as well as a strong attraction toward him.

After leaving Beauplan, Lysandre rescues Caliste's aged father Dorilas from a dozen attackers in the Forest of Fontainebleau but rides on without revealing his identity. At Fontainebleau, he manages to bring about a reconciliation when involved as his friend Clairange's second in a duel arising from a dispute with Caliste's brother Lydian over the affections of Olinde. To avoid prosecution for duelling, Clairange and Lysandre ride off to Paris and Lydian proceeds in high spirits to Beauplan.

Second Book. At Beauplan, Lydian's praise for Lysandre's mediation is soon reinforced by that of Dorilas upon discovering his rescuer's identity. The only person not enthusiastically grateful to Lysandre is Béronte, who knows the true objetc of such services. Meanwhile, Lysandre decides to test Caliste's gratitude by requesting a secret rendezvous in a letter delivered by means of a village woman and Caliste's attendant Clarinde, both previously cultivated by him for such services. Despite honor-dictated misgivings, Caliste reluctantly sends permission for him to visit her alone late the following night in Cléandre's absence. Only the shrewdness of Lysandre's Basque valet prevents the discovery of this clandestine correspondence in an accidental encounter with Cléandre and others near Beauplan. The rendezvous itself is imperiled by Cléandre's unexpected return to Beauplan, but Lysandre is received in Caliste's bedroom after a stealthy entry into the house. Lysandre's discomfiture at learning of the unexpected crisis is compounded by Cléandre's unforeseen visit to Caliste's room to report a nightmare in which she had been abducted by a dragon. Having remained successfully concealed during the hour of Cléandre's amorous call, Lysandre is frustrated in his open, passionate attempt to seduce Caliste in her bed when she angrily summons Clarinde. Leaving in disgrace, he accidentally drops a pistol which discharges and awakens the household. Barely able to elude pursuing servants and dogs, he manages to reach his waiting horse and escape to Paris.

Third Book. The disturbance is dismissed at Beauplan as a frustrated robbery attempt. After Dorilas' good offices have obtained a royal pardon for the recent duel at Fontainebleau, its participants Lysandre, Clairange, Lydian, and Alcidon come to visit Beauplan; but the otherwise cordial Caliste refuses to have any private communication with Lysandre. Discouraged, he decides to go to Rimbergue in Holland to assist Prince Maurice against Spinola. To Caliste's chagrin, all the gentlemen at Beauplan accompany Lysandre on this expedition, which provides him many opportunities for glorious exploits. Returning to Paris, Lysandre and his friends reveal their identity after initiating a "champ ouvert" combat in the Arsenal square in the King's presence, a contest soon stopped upon the wounding of the royal favorite Cloridan by Lysandre. After a banquet that evening at Cléandre's town house, Caliste breaks off an awkward discussion of Lysandre's mysterious love-life by asking him to sing. Accompanying himself on the lute, he sings his own verses, addressed to an imaginary "Ypolite". Summoned outside by a page, he is attacked by four men who seriously wound him before they are killed by Cléandre and other guests. Although physicians declare each of Lysandre's wounds to be fatal, Lydian avails himself of the reputedly miraculous healing powers of an *opérateur*, who needs only to have Lysandre's torn and bloody doublet brought to him to cause the absent Lysandre's wounds to close and his bleeding to stop. It is soon discovered that the ambush had been organized by a vengeful cousin of Cloridan, who is as appalled as everyone else at the incident. The King urges that the conspirators' death be considered adequate retribution.

Fourth Book. During Lysandre's convalescence, the bitter rivalry of Clairange and Lydian over Olinde is renewed. When Olinde's preferential treatment of Lydian results in a crisis, she promises her affection to whichever suitor will be the latter to appear before her again, a pronouncement which brings about the disconsolate departure of both rivals. Although Lysandre's gradual recovery has bean hastened by his nurse Caliste's equivocal indication of imminent complaisance, his second unsuccessful seduction attempt reveals that she has no intention of submitting to him physically at any time. After angrily denouncing her hypocrisy and receiving the calm acknowledgement of her debt to him, Lysandre takes leave of his hosts and journeys to the home of his sister Ambrise in Burgundy, where he falls violently ill upon arriving.

Meanwhile, having gone to Italy on business, Cléandre has occasion to help the ghost of the murdered landlord of a haunted inn and receives the grateful ghost's promise to repay this service by warning him three days in advance of his death.

In Burgundy, after physicians have despaired of his recovery, Lysandre astounds a delegation of local Capuchin monks at his presumed deathbed by vomiting forth a supernatural array of unlikely objects. When exhorted to accept death as a blessing by a handsome and unusually sorrowful young monk, the revived Lysandre recognizes Clairange, who explains the vomiting as a result of the *opérateur*'s demonic charm and tells of his own decision to withdraw to the peace of the monastic life. Vowing to make a pilgrimage of thanksgiving to Montserrat in Spain, Lysandre has a suitable costume made and sets out. News of this remarkable encounter brings Alcidon hurrying from Paris to Burgundy but arriving too late to see Lysandre and unable to dissuade Clairange from his vocation.

In the absence of her husband and most of her friends, the socially withdrawn Caliste is faced with a new problem in Clarinde's frequent bedroom assignations for Béronte's friend Léon. Caliste merely remonstrates with her, not realizing the misfortunes that will result from Clarinde's misconduct.

Fifth Book. Arriving at Montserrat, Lysandre soon encounters a group dressed as slaves and recognizes their leader as Cléandre, who is equally joyful at this reunion. Cléandre tells of his capture by Algerian pirates off Genoa while returning from Italy, his subsequent rescue in the Gulf of Barcelona, and his own pilgrimage of thanksgiving. The next day, the two friends discover that a famous young preacher-hermit addressing a great crowd is Lydian, whose discouragement in love had caused him to undertake this vocation. In view of Clairange's definitive withdrawal, Lydian is now free to return to his courtship of Olinde. Returning to France in their same Montserrat apparel, they visit Clairange to confirm his reconciliation with Lydian and take him along to Paris.

Meanwhile, after being dismissed by Caliste for her incorrigible behavior, the desperate and vindictive Clarinde succeeds in recovering her post by enlisting the support of Béronte, who wishes to retain her as an informant in a position to observe Caliste.

During an engagement ceremony for Alcidon and Argire, Lysandre, Cléandre, and Clairange enter unexpectedly and urge Olinde to send for Lydian, who will thus have fulfilled the requirement she had established. Upon her consent, Lydian enters and throws himself at her feet. Their engagement is then confirmed by a priest together with the scheduled one.

Sixth Book. Having reluctantly accepted Cloridan's unexpected and unwelcome challenge to a secret duel (despite an awkward medical indisposition), Lysandre kills Cloridan and mortally wounds his second Crisante but is seriously wounded himself. After Lysandre has taken refuge in Clairange's monastery cell in Paris, Béronte and Léon come upon the dying Crisante, who fully justifies Lysandre's conduct in the affair. After Léon has surreptitiously retrieved and concealed Lysandre's sword, the pair rides back into Paris to report the event. Cloridan's friends convince the King that Lysandre murdered his foe in ambush and obtain a royal pursuit order. Healed by one of the monks, Lysandre is conveyed secretly by his friends to Beauplan, where it is decided that he must seek temporary refuge in Flanders. Disconsolate at having left her lover behind in Paris, Clarinde arranges for an assignation at Beauplan, informing Léon of Lysandre's earlier method of entry.

Cléandre is now visited by the ghost of the Italian innkeeper, who notifies him of imminent death. Just before the expiration of the three-day period, the prematurely relieved Cléandre is killed by the unidentified Léon when the latter is trapped in a stairway by the retiring household and desperately rushes to safety. Having wrested Lysandre's sword from his assailant's hand before being stabbed, the dying Cléandre is perplexed but refuses to attribute such a crime to his friend and dies nobly after an eloquent farewell to Caliste. His visiting kinsman Varasque, taking charge in Béronte's absence, soon determines the killer's means af access and identifies Clarinde's footprints. When Clarinde brazenly claims to have opened the gate on Caliste's orders, judges are summoned, to whom Clarinde declares that she had unwillingly admitted Lysandre, her mistress' paramour, a liaison to which Béronte could attest if present. Caliste is immediately imprisoned in the Petit Châtelet in Paris to await trial.

Seventh Book. Returning from a visit to Lysandre's sister Ambrise in Burgundy and learning the news, Béronte is convinced of the truth of Clarinde's story, an apparent acknowledgement of Lysandre's cowardice which delights Cloridan's partisans and dismays Lysandre's. Hurrying secretly to his friends in Paris upon learning of the disaster, Lysandre explains the presence of his sword and begins to organize Caliste's hitherto neglected defense. In order to communicate with her, Lysandre rents an upstairs room in a butcher's house facing the Petit Châtelet across an alley and succeeds in tossing an encouraging letter and writing materials into Caliste's cell. Her reply is intercepted in the alley by a guard, but Lysandre manages to snatch it away and flee. His next letter to her instructs her to attempt to bribe her guard, whom she has already found to be willing to help her, as is her serving-woman. Informed of Lysandre's message, the guard meets him to arrange for Caliste's escape on Twelfth Night, the earliest possible opportunity. The escape takes place as planned when the prison officials have finally sunk into a drunken stupor after their holiday carousal, enabling the guard to escort Caliste and her serving-woman to her waiting friends after a terrifying delay.

Eighth Book. Alerted by prison authorities, the sternly conscientious plaintiff Varasque suspects the complicity of Caliste's friends in her escape. Warned of this by Béronte (secretly delighted at her escape though a plaintiff also), her friends decide upon her immediate flight to Brussels with Lysandre, a project to which she agrees with reluctance. After arriving in Brussels and patriotically refusing a pension from the Archduke, Lysandre is obliged to escape extradition by the French ambassador by fleeing with Caliste to Frisia. It is at this time that Caliste acknowledges his devotion and her own love with a promise of marriage upon their final vindication.

In Paris, meanwhile, Béronte and Lydian are persuaded by their friends to set out to find the alleged key witness, Léon.

The unwelcome attentions for Caliste of an arrogant Frisian nobleman, Béranger, in addition to depleted financial resources, make the exiles decide to return to France in order to seek refuge in some as yet unconfiscated Gascon holding of Lysandre. After being forced to kill Béranger and his henchmen when waylaid at the Frisian border, Lysandre escorts Caliste safely back to France. Passing near her parents' estate, Lysandre visits it alone, disguised as a lackey messenger. Despite her mother's great indignation at Caliste's behavior in fleeing justice in the company of Cléandre's supposed murderer, Lyandre is able to convince her of the truth of the situation and persuades her to offer Caliste asylum while he returns to Paris. Near Saint-Germain, he rescues Caliste's former guard from a group of archers escorting him to prison and takes him to Gascony as a valet.

Meanwhile, Caliste's father has been able to persuade the King to pardon Lysandre for Cloridan's death and personally to investigate the murder of Cléandre, provided that Lysandre come to Paris within one month. Delighted to find Caliste awaiting him at his estate, Dorilas sends a messenger to Lysandre with letters informing him of the restoration of his good name, contingent upon his returning to Paris. However, the messenger's accidental drowning on the way leaves Lysandre ignorant of the pardon and its deadline.

Ninth Book. Having been joyfully received by his parents after a ten-year absence, Lysandre is soon aware of their efforts to marry him to Ypolite, a beautiful young Amazonian heiress living nearby. Although much impressed by her beauty, he remains faithful to Caliste and merely feigns interest in Ypolite, thereby winning her unsought love.

Meanwhile, Lysandre's failure to return to Paris has resulted in an appeal to the King by Lucidan (a kinsman of Cloridan's slain second who is secretly in love with Caliste) that his pardon be revoked and that satisfaction be given for the double "murder" of the duel. The King decress that unless Lysandre appears within an additional three weeks or is championed by a friend against Lucidan in public combat thereafter, the pardon will be revoked and the murder charge regularly prosecuted. After Lydian has been dispatched to Gascony to warn Lysandre, Caliste learns of the supposed affair between Lysandre and Ypolite. Convinced that this is none other than the Ypolite of Lysandre's song *(Third Book)* and overwhelmed by jealous grief, she disguises herself in her brother's clothes and slips away at night.

In Gascony, Lysandre avoids any commitment to Ypolite by leaving abruptly, ostensibly to go to Paris but actually to visit Caliste's parents' estate. But distracted in Bordeaux by news of a great tournament to be held in London, he embarks at once for England. Furious at his escape, his father is further dismayed to learn of the jeopardized pardon from Lydian, who in turn is lured to England while attempting to overtake Lysandre.

Meanwhile, the disguised Caliste has a suit of armor made for herself in Paris, intending to challenge Lucidan in order to humiliate both Lysandre and him by her death.

In London, obliged to wait until the last day of the tournament to take part, Lysandre defeats the champions of the day before and then overcomes another unexpected late contestant. The scene becomes one of happy reunion upon the discovery that the two previous champions are Alcidon and Béronte and that the latecomer is Lydian. After being presented King Arthur's sword and a collar of precious stones by King James's son and daughter, Lysandre politely refuses a royal pension. Following a triumphal reception for them at the palace, the four friends set out for Dover, where they embark for Calais despite storm warnings.

Having received Caliste's anonymous challenge to a secret duel, Lucidan refuses it, insisting on awaiting the royally sanctioned public encounter to be held on the site of the future Place Royale (Place des Vosges). On that occasion, however, both Caliste's father and Lysandre's father come forward as champion candidates, forcing the King to have lots drawn.

During a violent Channel storm, Lysandre becomes accidentally separated from his friends and is cast up in a skiff on the Jersey shore, where he encounters a young hermit loudly lamenting his past misdeeds. The other passengers finally reach Calais, and Lysandre's grieving friends set out for Paris with his belongings.

The drawing of lots is interrupted by the arrival of a fourth challenger, styled the "Knight of Lysandre", who wins the drawing and engages in fierce, well-matched combat with Lucidan. During the intermission following two hours of fighting, Béronte, Alcidon, and Lydian arrive and persuade the King to stop the combat. Finally convinced of Lysandre's innocence in the two duelling deaths, the King absolves him *in absentia* of any guilt in this connection, imposes eternal silence on Cloridan's partisans, and orders Lucidan to embrace the "Knight of Lysandre", who is revealed to be Ypolite and with whom Lucidan promptly falls in love. Having slipped away in despair at this apparent confirmation of the reported liaison between Lysandre and Ypolite, Caliste is followed by an officer whom the King has ordered to learn her identity.

Tenth Book. Learning of Caliste's whereabouts, Alcidon goes to her and tricks her into revealing her identity. Having persuaded her to resume feminine dress and to retire for propriety's sake to a nearby convent for the time being, he goes to inform the group of friends of this event. When the royal officer returns to Court with Caliste's abandoned horse and armor, Ypolite persuades the King to let her stand guard over them until they are claimed. A dramatic reunion is now brought about when friends and parents go to Caliste's convent refuge and then take her for presentation to the King and Queen, who are charmed by her. Ypolite is brought in to meet her, and the rivals exchange compliments despite the envy lurking in both women. Disturbed and humiliated by Caliste's apparent acceptance by Lysandre's father, Ypolite secretly dons Caliste's armor and departs.

On Jersey, recognizing the plaintive hermit to be León, Lysandre orders him to accompany him to Paris to confess having killed Cléandre, to which Léon agrees with good grace. While travelling from Le Havre to Paris, Lysandre encounters the disguised Ypolite, who is incorrectly identified for him as Caliste. His prompt explanation to her of his feigned love for Ypolite infuriates his interlocutor, who pretends to be Lucidan and claims to have slain Caliste in combat. Her wish to die at Lysandre's hands is almost fulfilled in the ensuing violent combat, but his last-minute recognition of her causes him to leave her wounded and unconscious as he retires in chagrin. Soon after, however, he is recalled to her bedside for an apology and pardon. As good friends, the two go to Paris with Léon, arriving spectacularly just as the militant plaintiff Varasque and Lysandre's father are about to engage in combat before the King, the Court, and all other interested persons. Léon's confession earns him banishment and Clarinde permanent confinement in the *Filles Repenties*. Lysandre and Caliste are restored to their original honorable status and are also awarded the confiscated property of the two criminals.

The apparent elimination of all obstacles to the protagonists' marriage is spoiled by Caliste's sudden and short-lived attitude of distaste toward Lysandre. Dismayed and resentful, he retires secretly to Mont Valérien near Paris to become a hermit, a blow which nearly kills Caliste, who slowly regains health but not happiness. After three months, Lysandre's enthusiasm for the hermit's life chills with the coming of winter. Hearing of Caliste's illness and of the imminent marriages of Alcidon and Lydian, he readily accepts his fellow hermits' advice to return to the world and Caliste. Arriving incognito in Paris, he reveals his presence to Caliste by singing outside her window but does not appear in public until the day of the lance contest sponsored by the Queen as part of the wedding festivities. Late in that contest, he appears as an unknown knight, wins a splendid triumph, and then reveals his identity, to the unanimous joy of the spectators. Although her coy and insincere reticence before the King nearly wrecks Caliste's long-awaited union with him, Lysandre saves it by appealing to her publicly for a definite commitment in regard to him. Caliste happily confirms her earlier promise of marriage.

The originally planned double wedding is expanded to include all five young couples, duly married the next morning in the presence of the King and Queen in the Bourbon Chapel of the Louvre.

The banquet is interrupted by the appearance of a nymph who creates a storm in the hall, making Lysandre and Caliste fear a new attempt to separate them. When the nymph and storm-cloud disappear, the guests see a black marble obelisk spouting forth water, which forces them to clamber onto the tables to avoid being drenched. When the flood recedes, they are able to examine prophetic inscriptions in Spanish, Italian, and Old French, which though enigmatic at the time are later understood to refer to the assassination of Henri IV, the regency of Marie de Médicis, and the unprecedented glory of young Louis XIII's reign. Taking this highly unusual occurrence in their stride, the guests enjoy a day of revelry and jousts, after which the brides and bridegrooms retire to partake of greater delights in a scene memorable for the somewhat prurient enthusiasm of the author in describing it.

4. *Les Diverses Affections de Minerve*

> MINERVE, young noblewoman married unhappily in Louis XIII's reign.
> ADRASTE, penurious young knight in love with Minerve.
> TATIUS, Parisian magistrate, later Minerve's second husband.
> CRASSUS, Adraste's ugly but crafty rival.
> ARNOULPHE, boorish young foreigner loved by Minerve.
> CARICLÉE, Minerve's rival for Adraste's affection.

Chapter I. The daughter of an illustrious family, having lost her father while still an infant, the clever, attractive Minerve was married at the age of nine to a boy of eleven. After several years of complete incompatibility, Minerve comes to Paris to sue for annulment. While her suit is underway, she receives the attentions of many admirers but shows favor only to the ugly Crassus, the uncourtly foreigner Arnoulphe, and the sensitive, penurious young knight Adraste, who is particularly disturbed by an awareness of someone else's successful competition. Moved spontaneously to serenade her one evening, Adraste and several friends become involved in a street fight with ruffians outside the Porte St-Germain. Dispersing these, Adraste imprudently routs a second group, made up of comedians and prominent jurists, a mistake which brings about the first stages of legal prosecution the next day.

Chapter II. After Minerve uses her good offices to have the complaint dismissed, she persuades Adraste to accept the fact of her irrational preference of Arnoulphe and to become her confidant. Soon after, she is unwillingly obliged to marry her attorney, old Senator Tatius, in return for a substantial loan which has enabled her to win her annulment suit; for Arnoulphe has been killed in a duel and Adraste is still dependent on his father. Although the marriage (necessitating a great financial sacrifice for Tatius) is at first clandestine, Minerve's pregnancy soon exposes the union, which results in the birth of two children and the evaporation of Tatius' fortune before Minerve goes again to Paris to seek a property separation, annulment itself no longer being possible.

Chapter III. Re-establishing contact with Adraste, Minerve soon learns of his complete devotion to her, a frustrating situation for both because of her married status. Their liaison is troubled by other admirers of hers, one of whom exploits his kinship in seeking her company. A bloody quarrel between Adraste and two rivals is barely averted during a walk in the Tuileries gardens. Their continued attentions for Minerve cause the jealous Adraste to break off his relationship with her by means of a bitter letter.

Chapter IV. Disturbed at this rupture, Minerve effects a wan reconciliation with Adraste but learns of the existence of a rival, Cariclée. After composing poetry at Minerve's request to commemorate Arnoulphe's death, Adraste leaves to take part in Louis XIII's Normandy campaign (1621). Tatius has become involved in a seditious political intrigue, is disgraced, and involves the complaisant Minerve in the heavy debts which result. In Adraste's absence, Minerve allows Crassus to re-establish himself in her favor. Adraste accompanies the royal army from Normandy to Le Mans and takes part in the storming of Pont de Cé despite the handicap of an infected leg wound.

Chapter V. After taking part in the pacification of Guyenne and the restoration of Roman Catholic privileges in Béarn, Adraste returns to Paris with the Court and promptly falls gravely ill. Cariclée's solicitude at this time erases his affection for her rival temporarily, but Minerve is later able to rekindle his passion for her after insisting that he call on her.

Chapter VI. Unable to arouse jealousy in Adraste to intensify his passion by revealing to him the attentions of his rival Crassus, Minerve abruptly forbids him to pay her further evening visits after he is waylaid and slightly wounded while walking to her house.

Chapter VII. Having decided to accompany the royal expedition against the Huguenot assembly at La Rochelle, Adraste is persuaded by Minerve to delay his departure but is displeased at several indications of Crassus' influence over her as well as at the lukewarm qualities of her pledges of love to him during a trip to the Rueil gardens.

Chapter VIII. The author reveals that Crassus is covertly engaged in making Minerve obligated to him as she had been to Tatius. Meanwhile, Adraste performs timely services for her, lending her his horse for a sudden trip to see her sick mother and punishing an unruly tenant farmer. She displays her gratitude in confiding to him how Tatius had recently cajoled her into intercourse, hoping malevolently for a pregnancy which he could publicly disclaim.

Chapter IX. During a walk together, Minerve unexpectedly orders Adraste to curtail his visits to her to avoid scandal. Furious, Adraste is ready to challenge Crassus but then decides merely to leave at once for the King's service without seeing Minerve again.

Chapter X. Touched in spite of himself by Minerve's affectionate farewell note delivered on the eve of his departure, Adraste goes at once to visit her and is received in her bedroom, where he stays until dawn in intimate conversation. After a few hours' sleep at home, he returns to continue their conversation, with Minerve lying dove-like in his arms until the moment of their fond leave-taking in mid-afternoon. At this point, the author promises an even more pleasant and heroic continuation of Adraste's adventures in the non-existent second part of the novel.

5. *Les Amours d'Aristandre et de Cléonice*

    LYSIDOR, Sophy of Persia.
    ALBANIE, Queen of Persia.
    ARISTANDRE, young Persian courtier.
    ALCANDRE, Aristandre's older brother and Lysidor's chief minister.

CLÉONICE, young lady-in-waiting to Albanie and Aristandre's beloved.
ARSILÉE, officious chief lady-in-waiting.
LÉONIDE, lady-in-waiting for whom Aristandre feigns love.
MARIANNE, "Hiberian" lady-in-waiting in whom Aristandre also feigns interest
Story I
HIPARQUE, famous Persian clergyman and preacher
EURIGÈNE, object of Hiparque's secret lust.
LICIDAS, Eurigène's husband and Hiparque's devoted admirer.
Story II
POLINICE, young Babylonian.
HÉLISE, Polinice's beloved.
PALMIRE, Polinice's devoted friend.
ICARE, Polinice's unscrupulous rival, killed by him.
PALOMBE, magician who helps Icare and later Polinice.
Story III
MARTHÉSIE, Queen Mother of Persia.
BOHÉMONT, Marthésie's devoted courtier.
TISSAFERNE, Bohémont's valorous but arrogant friend.
SILÉSIE, lady-in-waiting to Marthésie and Tissaferne's beloved.
Story IV
TIRIBASE, brave but prodigal young knight.
ORITHIE, Tiribase's beloved.
PHILÉTAS, Orithie's rich but miserly merchant father.

First Book. In the city of Persepolis, the court of the young Sophy of Persia, Lysidor, and his queen, Albanie, is graced by the presence of a handsome young courtier, Aristandre, and the object of his secret devotion, the beautiful young lady-in-waiting Cléonice. Aware of his love, she insists on concealing her own affection for him by feigning interest in other suitors. One of these is defeated in an illegal duel by Aristandre for having slandered his elder brother, Alcandre, the Sophy's chief minister. Aristandre's courtship of Cléonice is troubled by the interference of an officious busybody, Arsilée, chief lady-in-waiting, who persuades the Queen to forbid private conversations between the two and supports her argument as to the danger of such relationships by telling Albanie the story of a supposedly recent occurrence in Persepolis.

Story I. Although famous for his unrivaled success as a preacher, the clergyman Hiparque is not able to resist falling in love with the beautiful Eurigène, wife of his great admirer Licidas. Disturbed by Hiparque's ensuing campaign of seduction, Eurigène attemps to convince the incredulous Licidas of his friend's perfidy. Finally, Licidas agrees to hide nearby while Eurigène determines the extent of Hiparque's amorous designs. However, unknown to her, the wily preacher places a charm on Licidas and the whole household, plunging them into a deep slumber while he attempts to have his way with her. Realizing at the last moment that no help will be forthcoming, the desperate Eurigène is forced to stab Hiparque with his own dagger and tosses his corpse from the window into the street, where it is discovered by the watch and quickly traced to her room. Believing her story, the captain of the watch inquires at the preacher's monastery and soon discovers the nature of Hiparque's spell. In order not to damage the local high opinion of the clergy, the unfaithful preacher's body is buried secretly.

Second Book. Realizing the nature of Arsilée's grudge, the Queen discreetly orders Arsilée's assistant to monitor the conduct of her charges but to give Cléonice as much freedom as the others. Aristandre suffers temporary banishment from Cléonice's favor for having had a lock of her hair acquired surreptitiously for him. After his pardon, their reunion is marred by Arsilée's discovery of a diamond ring and a love-letter in Cléonice's possession, as well as other evidence of communication. When the Queen claims to see nothing amiss in Cléonice's acceptance of such a ring, Arsilée promptly tells her a story to prove the great danger inherent in ring-giving.

Story II. During the Queen's own reign, a young citizen of Babylon, Polinice, has suffered from his unrequited love for Hélise. While returning to Babyon from an adventure trip, he rescues his best friend, Palmire, from a crossroads ambush, killing among the assailants a rival suitor, Icare, who had previously obtained a magic ring from the magician Palombe in order to win Hélise and who was attempting to prevent Palmire from reporting this to his friend. Polinice removes the ring from Icare's body and goes on into the city with Palmire, who soon persuades Hélise to accept Polinice.

On their wedding day, Hélise first wears the magic ring, then replaces it with a finer ring presented to her by Polinice. During an after-supper ball game, Polinice places the magic ring on the finger of a nearby bronze statue of Venus. When he is later unable to remove the ring and decides to hammer it off, it disappears. That night and the two following nights, the spectre of a woman appears and prevents the consummation of the marriage.

Disturbed by his friend's rapidly failing health, Palmire persuades him to visit Palombe, who reluctantly advises Polinice to appear at the same crossroads in the nude at midnight to deliver a letter from the magician to a young man seated on a chariot-borne throne. Despite his fear, Polinice follows these instructions. The enthroned young man is annoyed to receive Polinice's request but instructs the nearby shade of Icare to escort Polinice to a gauze-clad figure riding a mule in the league-long procession of shades. The figure is the phantom who reluctantly gives up the magic ring just before the procession vanishes. Polinice returns home and thereafter enjoys untroubled connubial bliss.

Third Book. The Queen's only reaction to the story is to counsel Cléonice to be more discreet. In a questionable effort to distract the Court from his love for Cléonice, Aristandre becomes involved in cynically contrived decoy affairs with the trusting Léonide, daughter of the Sophy's former nurse, and later with the equally unsuspecting "Hiberian" lady-in-waiting Marianne, who becomes vindictive in her humiliation. When Cléonice suddenly falls ill, both Léonide and Marianne are used by Arsilée in an effort to have Cléonice sent home with royal consent, reluctantly given by the Sophy and his queen on the basis of Arsilée's feigned solicitude for the girl's health. While arrangements are being made for Cléonice's departure, the exultant Arsilée has the Queen told a story intended to convince her of the wisdom of this action.

Story III. During the reign of the present Sophy's father, the court of Queen Marthésie enjoyed the highest ideals and the presence of the finest people in the realm, in particular the noble Bohémont and the beautiful Silésie. Bohémont unwisely commends to the Queen's protection his valiant but excessively proud compatriot Tissaferne, whom she agrees to shelter from the Sophy's justice in an attractive sort of house arrest in her palace. The prisoner-guest escapes punishment for his unauthorized attentions to Silésie only by swearing his innocence and promising to avoid the ladies-in-waiting thereafter. The Queen orders Bohémont to inform Silésie of Tissaferne's unlawful participation in an incipient vendetta, which has resulted in his killing two of three brothers. In the midst of Bohémont's conversation with Silésie, the sudden arrival of the third brother causes Tissaferne to begin a duel in the Queen's own garden. The foes are arrested but soon released through Bohémont's good offices.

The Queen soon learns of Tissaferne's nocturnal visits to Silésie's quarters and personally apprehends the pair *en flagrant délit*, precipitating an unpleasant scene with Tissaferne, who leaves the palace in a rage. When Bohémont resists Tissaferne's efforts to involve him in his complaint about the Queen, he is compelled to engage in a duel with him, which is averted at the last moment by the arrival of the Queen's household with orders to seize and kill Tissaferne.

Bohémont's complicity in Tissaferne's subsequent escape deprives him of the Queen's favor and trust. When she summons Silésie's father, a satrap, to take his daughter away, the insulted father reacts in such a way as to bring about his own disgrace as well as that of Silésie. Queen Marthésie is chagrined not to have realized the danger of the situation before Tissaferne's intimacy with Silésie became too great.

Fourth Book. This story apparently has the desired effect on Queen Albanie, for Aristandre is hard put to devise a scheme to prevent Cléonice's departure. However, he does succeed in this by having the Sophy persuaded that a powerful foreign kinsman of Cléonice is alarmed at her apparently dishonorable dismissal. When the Sophy agrees to retain her at Court if her mother consents, Aristandre then has the mother warned of imaginary gossip (reputedly initiated by Arsilée) attributing Cléonice's departure to pregnancy, which makes the outraged mother determined to keep her daughter at Court for a year if necessary to disprove the slander. Upon the Aristandre-inspired advice of his spiritual counselor, the Sophy orders Cléonice to remain, a decision which delights the Queen. Soon after, Arsilée is persuaded to cease her persecution of the two lovers and thereafter allows them untroubled communication.

But their bliss is shortlived, for *raison d'Etat* causes the Sophy and Alcandre to choose a rich heiress as Aristandre's future bride. Despite his initial stubbornness, Aristandre soon submits gracefully to the royal will as a dutiful subject, as does the heartbroken Cléonice. As Aristandre and Cléonice exchange farewells as lovers, they are joined by a group of their friends, one of whom (a physiognomist) offers a prediction as to Cléonice's eventual marriage.

This prediction elicits a story from another friend about a remarkable case of clairvoyance.

Story IV. In Persepolis, the valiant but prodigal knight Tiribase is unable to win the hand of Orithie from her wealthy but miserly old merchant father Philétas. With the remainder of his sadly dissipated patrimony and with money lent by friends, Tiribase has two pirate ships outfitted and prepares to go seek his fortune. Before leaving he receives an elaborate prophecy from an Arab: Tiribase's misery will be far greater on land than at sea; he will acquire great riches at sea without possessing them; he will undergo great perils but will not perish; his greatest peril and greatest good fortune will be found in water but not at sea; great adversity and great prosperity await him; he will achieve his desire when hope is at its lowest ebb.

At first, Tiribase has excellent luck as a privateer attacking only other pirates, but a great storm on the Caspian Sea appears to sink all his ships while casting him up destitute on shore. Returning home, he attempts to trick Philétas into granting him Orithie by appearing in expensive clothes and pretending that his fleet is anchored safely nearby.

When Philétas discovers this ruse after agreeing to the marriage, he has Tiribase arrested for fraud in front of the old merchant's house. After a long farewell to Orithie, Tiribase plunges into a nearby well and Orithie flings herself from a window, landing unharmed. Pulled out of the well, Tiribase is found to be wearing a priceless jewelled collar, identified as the property of his family which a runaway slave had stolen and cast into the well years before.

As Tiribase and Orithie are recovering from shock, word comes of the authentic safe arrival of Tiribase's treasure-laden fleet. Chagrined at his own behavior, Philétas receives Tiribase's pardon, and the wedding takes place with great solemnity and magnificence.

APPENDIX B

A CONSOLIDATED BIBLIOGRAPHY OF THE PUBLISHING HISTORY OF D'AUDIGUIER'S *HISTOIRE TRAGE-COMIQUE DE NOSTRE TEMPS, SOUS LES NOMS DE LYSANDRE ET DE CALISTE*

References cited:

- A. AUBERT, p. xxi.
- AT. ARDENNE DE TIZAC, p. 142 f.
- B. BARBIER, p. 55 f.
- G. *Gesamtkatalog der preussischen Bibliotheken* (14 vols; Berlin: Preussischen Druckerei- und Verlags- Aktiengesellschaft, 1931-39), VIII, 209 f.
- H. HAINSWORTH, Les "*Novelas exemplares*", p. 246 f.
- J. S. PAUL JONES, *A List of French Prose Fiction from 1700 to 1750* (New York: The H. W. Wilson Co., 1939), p. 55.
- L. LACHÈVRE, *Les Recueils collectifs*, p. 159.
- M. MORÉRI, p. 500.
- P. PROCACCI, p. 220.
- VW. VON WURZBACH, p. 279 f.
- FV. This symbol indicates that the edition was consulted directly in the preparation of this study.

French editions:

- 1615. Paris: T. du Bray [*Tragi-comique**] (B, H, L).
- 1616. Paris: T. du Bray (AT, G, H, L, VW, FV).
- 1620. Paris: T. du Bray (H, L, VW).
- 1622. Paris: M. Collet (H).
- 1622. Paris: de la Vigne (G).
- 1622. Lyon (A) [*Histoire tragique**] (M).
- 1624. Paris: Antoine Bourriquet (AT, H, L).
- 1625. Paris: Veuve M. Guillemot (AT, H).
- 1626. Paris: T. du Bray (L).
- 1626. Lyon: Rigaud (G).
- 1628. Paris (H, VW).
- 1630. Rouen: Cailloué (G).
- 1633. Paris: Nicolas Gasse (G, FV).

1633. Lyon: Huguetan (AT, H, L, FV).
1637. Rouen: Cailloué (H, L, VW).
1645. Rouen: Cailloué (AT, G, H, L, VW).
1657. Amsterdam: Ravestein (H, VW).
1659. Amsterdam: Ravestein (G, H, L, VW).
1667. Paris: Bobin et Legras [*Histoire comique**] (AT, G, H, L).
1679. Amsterdam: H. et Th. Boem (G, H).
1707. Bruxelles (H).
1735. [Revised, modernized version by Guillot de la Chassagne entitled *Le Chevalier des Essars, et la Comtesse de Berci*] Amsterdam: Wetstein et Smith (G, J, FV).
1735. [*Ibid.*] Amsterdam: L'Honoré (H, J).
1735. [*Ibid.*] Paris: DuMesnil (J).
1735. [*Ibid.*] Paris: de Nully [DuMesnil] (J).
1735. [*Ibid.*] Paris: Huart (J).
1735. [*Ibid.*] Paris: Clouard (J).
1735. [*Ibid.*] Paris: Didot (J).
1750. [*Ibid.*] (J) Amsterdam: L'Honoré (H).
1785. [Condensation of original version in *Bibliothèque universelle des Romans*, mars 1785, 3-90] (FV).
1799. [Condensation of Guillot de la Chassagne's version in *Nouvelle Bibliothèque des romans*, 2e année, V (Paris: 1799), 58-127] (J, FV).

French-Dutch bilingual editions:

1650. Leyden: P. Leffer (H, VW).
1663. Amsterdam: Ravestein (G**, L, VW).
1663. Amsterdam: Boeckholt (B, L).
1670. Amsterdam: Ravestein (L).

English translation (A Tragi-Comicall History of Our Times, under the borrowed names of Lisander, And Calista):

1621. London (H).
1627. London (H): G. Lathum (FV).
1635. London (H): G. Lathum (FV).
1652. London (H).

Dutch translation (De treurige doch bly-eyndigende Historie van onsen tijdt):

1632. Amsterdam: Heerman (H, VW).
1636. Amsterdam: Heerman (G).
1658. Amsterdam: Boeckholt (G).
1665. Amsterdam (AT).
1669. Amsterdam: Heerman (H, VW).
1703. Amsterdam (H, VW).

APPENDIX B 161

German translation (Die traurige jedoch froelich-aussgehende Historia von Lysandern und Kalisten):

1644. Leyden (H, VW): Marci (G).
1644. Amsterdam: Elzevier [*Liebes-beschriebung Lysanders und Kalisten**] (G).
1650. Amsterdam (AT, H): Elzevier [*Liebes-beschreibung Lysanders und Kalisten**] (G, VW).
1670. [Bilingual] Amsterdam (B, H, VW): Ravestein [*Liebes beschreibung Lysanders und Kalisten, geschehen in Franckreich, meistenteils in und bei Paris, im Jahr 1606**] (G).

Italian translation (Gli amori di Lisandro e Calista):

1663. Venice: Storti (H, P).
1671. Venice (AT, H): Storti (P) e Pancirutti (G).

---

* Variation in title.
** Does not indicate bilingual edition.

BIBLIOGRAPHY OF WORKS CONSULTED

A. *Primary Sources*

AUDIGUIER, VITAL D', (SIEUR DE LA MENOR). *Les Amours d'Aristandre et de Cleonice.* Paris: R. Boutonné, 1626.

———. *Les Diverses Affections de Minerve, Avec une apologie d'elle-mesme. Et une Palynodie de l'autheur, et les epistres et libres discours du Sieur D'Audiguier.* Paris: Veuve M. Guillemot et M. Guillemot, 1625.

———, trans. *Les Diverses Fortunes de Panfile et de Nise. Où sont contenuës plusieurs Amoureuses et veritables histoires, tirees du pelerin en son pays de Lopé de Vega.* Paris: T. du Bray, 1614.

———. *Les Douces Affections de Lydamant et de Callyante.* Paris: T. du Bray, 1607.

———. *La Flavie de la Menor.* Paris: T. du Bray, 1606.

———. "Histoire des amours de Lysandre et de Caliste" [condensation of *Histoire trage-comique de nostre temps, sous les noms de Lysandre et de Caliste*], *Bibliothèque universelle des romans,* mars 1785, 3-90.

———. *Histoire trage-comique de nostre temps, sous les noms de Lysandre et de Caliste.* Paris: T. du Bray, 1616.

———. *Histoire trage-comique de nostre temps. Sous les noms de Lysandre et de Caliste.* Paris: Nicolas Gasse, 1633.

———. *Love and Valour: Celebrated in the person of the Author, by the name of Adraste. One part of the unfained story of Lisander and Calista. Out of the French by W. B[arwick].* London: T. Harper for T. Slater, 1638.

———. *Les Oeuvres poëtiques du Sieur Daudiguier.* Paris: T. du Bray, 1614.

———. *La Philosophie Soldade, avec un manifeste de l'autheur.* Paris: T. du Bray, 1604.

———. *Le Pourtrait du Monde.* París: T. du Bray, 1604.

———. *A Tragi-Comicall History of our times, under the borrowed names of Lisander, And Calista.* [Translated by W. Duncombe.] London: George Lathum, 1627.

———. *A Tragi-Comicall History of our times, under the borrowed names of Lisander, and Calista.* [Translated by W. Duncombe.] London: George Lathum, 1635.

———. *Le Vray et ancien usage des duels. Confirmé par l'exemple des plus illustres combats et deffys qui se soient faits en la chrestienté.* Paris: C. Billaine, 1617.

AUDIGUIER, VITAL D', (SIEUR DE LA MENOR), AND ROSSET, FRANÇOIS DE, trans. *Les Nouvelles de Michel Cervantes.* Paris: Jean Richer, 1621.

B. *Secondary Sources*

ADAM, ANTOINE. "Baroque et Préciosité", *Revue des sciences humaines,* 1949 (nos. 53-56), 208-224.

——. *Histoire de la littérature française au XVIIe siècle.* 5 vols. Paris: Domat-Montchrestien, 1948-56.

ARDENNE DE TIZAC, GEORGES D'. *Etude historique et littéraire sur Vital d'Audiguier, Seigneur de la Menor au pays de Rouergue.* Villefranche de Rouergue: Prosper Dufour, 1887.

ARIOSTO, LUDOVICO. *Orlando furioso.* Edited by Pietro Papini. Firenze: Sansoni, 1916.

AUBERT, PIERRE. "Bibliothèque du Richelet." In *Le Dictionnaire françois de Pierre Richelet.* Vol. I. Paris: J. Estienne, 1728.

"AUDIGUIER, VITAL D', (SEIGNEUR DE LA MENOR)." *Nouvelle Biographie générale depuis les temps les plus reculés jusqu'à nos jours.* Edited by J. C. F. Hoefer. Paris: Didot, 1855-66. III, 604.

BALTEAU, J. "Vital d'Audiguier." *Dictionnaire de biographie française.* Vol. IV. Paris: Librairie Letouzey et Ané, 1948.

BALZAC, JEAN-LOUIS GUEZ, SIEUR DE. *Socrate chrétien.* In *Oeuvres.* Edited by L. Moreau. Vol. II. Paris: Lecoffre, 1854.

BARBIER, ANTOINE-ALEXANDRE. *Examen critique et complément des dictionnaires les plus répandus depuis le Dictionnaire de Moréri, jusqu'à la Biographie universelle inclusivement.* Paris: Rey et Gravier, 1820.

BARDON, MAURICE. *"Don Quichotte" en France au XVIIe et au XVIIIe siècle: 1604-1815.* Tome I. Vol. LXIX of "Bibliothèque de la Revue de littérature comparée". Paris: Librairie ancienne Honoré Champion, 1931.

BARROUX, ROBERT. "Audiguier (Vital d')." *Dictionnaire des lettres françaises: le XVIIe siècle.* Paris: Librairie Arthème Fayard, 1954.

BAUM, PAULL FRANKLIN. "The Young Man Betrothed to a Statue", *Publications of the Modern Language Association,* XXXIV (1919), 523-79.

BAYLE, PIERRE. "Audiguier." *Dictionnaire historique et critique.* 5e édition. Amsterdam: P. Brunel, 1740-53. I, 381 f.

BICHLMAIER, KARL. *Die Preziosität der sentimentalen Romane des Sieur des Escuteaux.* Wertheim a. R.: Bechstein, 1931.

BOILEAU, NICOLAS. *L'Art poétique.* Cambridge: The University Press, 1931.

BONNEFON, PAUL. "Contribution à un essai de restitution du manuscrit de Guillaume Colletet intitulé *Vies des poètes françois*". *Revue d'histoire littéraire de la France,* II (1895), 59-77.

BOSSUAT, ROBERT. *Manuel bibliographique de la littérature française du Moyen Age.* Melun: Librairie d'Argences, 1951.

BOURGEOIS, EMILE, ET ANDRÉ, LOUIS. *Les Sources de l'histoire de France: XVIIe siècle (1610-1715).* Vol. IV: Journaux et pamphlets ["Manuels de bibliographie historique: Les Sources de l'histoire de France depuis les origines jusqu'en 1815", part III, vol. XIV]. Paris: August Picard, 1924.

BRAY, RENÉ. *La Formation de la doctrine classique en France.* Paris: Hachette, 1927.

BRERETON, GEOFFREY. *An Introduction to the French Poets: Villon to the Present Day.* Fair Lawn, N. J.: Essential Books, Inc., 1957.

British Museum Catalogue of Printed Books: 1881-1900. Ann Arbor: J. W. Edwards, 1946. Vols. III and XLVII.

BRUNET, JACQUES-CHARLES. *Manuel du libraire et de l'amateur de livres.* Paris: Firmin-Didot, 1860-65 [facsimile reprint; Berlin: Altmann, 1921-22]. Vol. V.

———. *Manuel du libraire et de l'amateur de livres. Supplément par MM. P. Deschamps et G. Brunet.* Paris: Firmin-Didot, 1878-80 [facsimile reprint; Paris: Dorbon-Aîné, 1928]. Vol. II.

Catalogue des livres composant la bibliothèque de feu M. le Baron James de Rothschild. Edited by Picot. Tomes I and II. Paris: Damascène Morgand, 1884-87.

Catalogue général des livres imprimés de la Bibliothèque Nationale: Auteurs. Tome V. Paris: Paul Catin, 1924.

Catalogue of Books Represented by Library of Congress Printed Cards. Ann Arbor: Edwards Brothers, Inc., 1942-46 (with supplements covering the period August 1948-December 1955 and continued since January 1956 by the *National Union Catalogue*).

CERVANTES SAAVEDRA, MIGUEL DE. *El Ingenioso Hidalgo Don Quixote de la Mancha.* Edited by Francisco Rodríguez Marín. Madrid: Ediciones Atlas, 1947-49.

———. *Novelas ejemplares.* Buenos Aires: Editorial Araujo, 1939.

CHIAPPELLI, FREDI. "Clorinda", *Studi Tassiani*, IV (1954), 19-22.

COLLETET, GUILLAUME. *Vie des poètes bordelais et périgourdins.* Edited by Tamizey de Larroque. Paris: Claudin, 1873.

CROOKS, ESTHER J. *The Influence of Cervantes in France in the 17th Century.* Vol. IV of "Johns Hopkins Studies in Romance Languages and Literatures". Baltimore: Johns Hopkins Press, 1931.

DEIERKAUF-HOLSBOER, S. WILMA. "Vie d'Alexandre Hardy, poète du roi", *Proceedings of the American Philosophical Society*, XCI (1947), no. 4, 328-404.

DOUTREPONT, GEORGES. *Jean Lemaire de Belges et la Renaissance.* Bruxelles: Hayez, 1934.

DUNLOP, JOHN COLIN. *The History of Fiction: being a critical account of the most celebrated prose works of fiction from the earliest Greek romances to the novels of the present age.* 3rd edition. London: Longman, 1845.

DU RYER, PIERRE. *Lisandre et Caliste.* Paris: Pierre David, 1632.

FAGNIEZ, GUSTAVE. *La Femme et la société française dans la première moitié du XVIIe siècle.* Paris: J. Gamber, 1929.

Gesamtkatalog der preussischen Bibliotheken mit Nachweis des identischen Besitzes der Bayerischen Staatsbibliothek in München und der Nationalbibliothek in Wien. Herausgegeben von der Preussischen Staatsbibliothek. Berlin: Preussische Druckerie- und Verlags- Aktiengesellschaft, 1931-39. Vol. VIII.

GOUJET, CLAUDE-PIERRE. *Bibliothèque françoise, ou, Histoire de la littérature françoise.* Paris: Mariette, 1740-56.

GREEN, F. C. "The Critic of the seventeenth century and his attitude toward the French novel", *Modern Philology*, XXIV (1926-27), 285-95.

———. *French Novelists, Manners and Ideas, from the Renaissance to the Revolution.* New York: D. Appleton and Co., 1931.

GREIFELT, ROLF. "Die Übersetzungen des spanischen Schelmenromans in Frankreich im 17. Jahrhundert", *Romanische Forschungen*, L (1936), 51-84.

[GUILLOT DE LA CHASSAGNE, ABBÉ IGNACE VINCENT]. *Le Crevalier des Essars, et la comtesse de Berci*. Amsterdam: Wetstein et Smith, 1735.

——. "Le Chevalier des Essars, et la comtesse de Berci" [condensation], *Nouvelle Bibliothèque des Romans*, 2e année, V [Paris: 1799], 58-127.

HAINSWORTH, GEORGE. "Cervantes en France: à propos de quelques publications récentes", *Bulletin hispanique*, XXXIV (1932), 128-44.

——. *Les "Novelas exemplares" de Cervantes en France au XVIIe siècle*. Vol. XCV of "Bibliothèque de la littérature comparée". Paris: Librairie ancienne Honoré Champion, 1933.

——. "Quelques notes sur la fortune de Lope de Vega en France (XVIIe siècle)", *Bulletin hispanique*, XXXIII (1931), 199-213.

HALL, JOSEPH. *The Discovery of a New World [Mundus alter et idem]*. Translated by John Healey. Edited by Huntington Brown. Cambridge: Harvard University Press, 1937.

HAMERTON, PHILIP G. *Paris in Old and Present Times*. London: Seeley, 1892.

HELIODORUS. *An Ethiopian Romance*. Translated by Moses Hadas. Ann Arbor: University of Michigan Press, 1957.

HUET, PIERRE-DANIEL. "De l'origine des romans." In La Fayette, Marie-Madeleine de la Vergne, comtesse de, *Oeuvres*. Paris: Garnier, 1864.

HUGUET, EDMOND. *Quomodo Jacobi Amyot sermonem quidam d'Audiguier emendaverit*. Paris: P. Noizette, 1894.

JACOUBET, H. "Sources", *Annales de l'Université de Grenoble (N. S.): Section Lettres-Droit*, XVII (1941), 247-57.

JOLY, PHILIPPE-LOUIS. "Audiguier (N. d')." *Remarques critiques sur le Dictionnaire de Bayle*. Première Partie: A-F. Paris: E. Ganeau (Lyon: François Desventes), 1752. Pp. 156-58.

JONES, S. PAUL. *A List of French Prose Fiction from 1700 to 1750*. New York: The H. W. Wilson Co., 1939.

KEATING, L. CLARK. *Studies on the Literary Salon in France: 1550-1615*. Vol. XVI of "Harvard Studies in Romance Languages". Cambridge: Harvard University Press, 1941.

KÖRTING, HEINRICH. *Geschichte des französischen Romans im 17. Jahrhundert*. 2. Ausgabe. Oppeln und Leipzig: Franck, 1891.

KÜCHLER, WALTHER. "Empfindsamkeit und Erzählungskunst im Amadisroman", *Zeitschrift fur französischen Sprache und Literatur*, XXXV, 158-225.

——. "Zu den Anfängen des psychologischen Romans in Frankreich", *Archiv für das Studium der neueren Sprachen und Literaturen*, CXXIII (1909), 88-118.

LACHÈVRE, FRÉDÉRIC. *Bibliographie des recueils collectifs de poésies publiés de 1597 à 1700*. Paris: H. Leclerc, 1901-05. Vol. I.

——. *Les Recueils collectifs de poésies libres et satiriques publiés depuis 1600 jusqu'à la mort de Théophile (1626)*. Vol. IV of "Le Libertinage au XVIIe siècle". Paris: Champion, 1914.

LANCASTER, H. C. *A History of French Dramatic Literature in the Seventeenth Century. Part I: The Pre-Classical Period (1610-1634)*. Baltimore and Paris: Johns Hopkins Press and Presses Universitaires de France, 1929.

——. "Pierre Du Ryer écrivain dramatique", *Revue d'histoire littéraire de la France*, XX (1913), 309-31.

LANSON, GUSTAVE. "Etudes sur les rapports de la littérature française et de la littérature espagnole au XVIIe siècle", *Revue d'histoire littéraire de la France*, III (1896), 45-70.

LANSON, GUSTAVE. "La Fonction des influences étrangères dans le développement de la littérature française", *Revue des Deux-Mondes*, 15 février 1917, 801-06.

———. "G. Reynier. *Le Roman sentimental avant l'Astrée* [compte rendu]", *Revue d'histoire littéraire de la France*, XVI (1909), 401.

———. *Histoire de la littérature française*. Paris: Hachette, 1920.

LE BRETON, ANDRÉ. *Le Roman au XVIIe siècle*. Paris: Hachette, 1890.

L'ESTOILE, PIERRE DE. "Mémoires pour servir à l'histoire de France et Journal de Henri III et de Henri IV." *Collection complète des mémoires relatifs à l'histoire de France*. Edited by Claude B. Petitot. Paris: Foucault, 1819-29. Vol. XLVII (Première Série).

L'HERMITE, FRANÇOIS-TRISTAN. *Le Page disgracié*. Edited by Auguste Dietrich. Paris: Librairie Plon, 1898.

LOMÉNIE, LOUIS DE. "La Littérature romanesque: I. Du roman en France jusqu'à l'Astrée", *Revue des Deux-Mondes*, 1er décembre 1857, 593-633; "II. L'Astrée et le roman pastoral", *Revue des Deux-Mondes*, 15 juillet 1858, 446-80; "III. Le Roman sous Louis XIII", *Revue des Deux-Mondes*, 1er février 1862, 722-49.

LOUANDRE, CHARLES. "Les Conteurs français au XVIIe siècle", *Revue des Deux-Mondes*, 1er mars 1874, 97-122.

MAGENDIE, MAURICE. *La Politesse mondaine et les théories de l'honnêteté en France au XVIIe siècle, de 1600 à 1660*. Paris: F. Alcan, 1925.

———. *Le Roman français au XVIIe siècle, de l'Astrée au Grand Cyrus*. Paris: E. Droz, 1932.

———. "Une 'source' inconnue du *Tartuffe*", *Revue des Deux-Mondes*, 15 juin 1929, 929-36.

MAGNE, EMILE. *La Vie quotidienne au temps de Louis XIII*. Paris: Hachette, 1942.

MAROT, CLÉMENT. *Oeuvres*. Edited by Georges Guiffrey. Vol. III. Paris: Morgand et Fatout, 1876.

MONGRÉDIEN, GEORGES. *La Vie littéraire au XVIIe siècle*. Paris: Tallandier, 1947.

MORÉRI, LOUIS. "Audiguier, Vital d'." *Le Grand Dictionnaire historique*. Edited by Drouet. Paris: Les Libraires associés, 1758-59. I, 499f.

MORILLOT, PAUL. *Le Roman en France depuis 1610 jusqu'à nos jours*. Paris: Masson, 1892.

PELLISSON-FONTANIER, PAUL, AND D'OLIVET, PIERRE-JOSEPH. *Histoire de l'Académie Française*. Edited by Ch.-L. Livet. Paris: Didier, 1858.

PLINY THE YOUNGER. *Letters*. Translated by William Melmoth and revised by W. M. L. Hutchinson for "Loeb Classical Library." London: William Heinemann, 1927.

POTTINGER, DAVID T. *The French Book Trade in the Ancien Régime: 1500-1791*. Cambridge: Harvard University Press, 1958.

PROCACCI, G. "Un romanzo francese del seicento e una sua traduzione italiana," *Bulletin italien*, VI (1906), 219-33.

RATEL, SIMONNE. "La Cour de la Reine Marguerite," *Revue du seizième siècle*, XI (1924), 1-29, 193-207; XII (1925), 1-43.

RATNER, MOSES. *Theory and Criticism of the Novel in France from L'Astrée to 1750*. New York: De Palma, 1938.

REURE, O.-C. *La Vie et les œuvres de Honoré d'Urfé.* Paris: Librairie Plon, 1910.
REYNIER, GUSTAVE. *Le Roman réaliste au XVIIe siècle.* Paris: Hachette, 1914.
———. *Le Roman sentimental avant l'Astrée.* Paris: Armand Colin, 1908.
ROCHEGUDE, MARQUIS DE, ET DUMOLIN, MAURICE. *Guide pratique à travers le vieux Paris.* Paris: Librairie ancienne Edouard Champion, 1923.
ROLFE, F. P. "On the bibliography of 17th century prose fiction", *Publications of the Modern Language Association,* XLIX (1934), 1071-86.
RONSARD, PIERRE DE. *Oeuvres complètes.* Edited by Paul Laumonier. Paris: Lemerre, 1914-19. Vol. III.
SAINT-AMANT, MARC-ANTOINE DE GÉRARD, sieur de. *Oeuvres complètes.* Edited by Ch.-L. Livet. Paris: Jannet, 1855. Vol. I.
SAINTSBURY, GEORGE. *A History of the French Novel (to the Close of the 19th Century).* Vol. I: From the Beginnings to 1800. London: Macmillan, 1917.
SOREL, CHARLES. *L'Anti-Roman ou l'Histoire du berger Lysis, accompagnée de ses remarques.* Paris: T. du Bray, 1633.
———. *La Bibliothèque françoise ou le choix et l'examen des livres françois.* Paris: Par la Compagnie des libraires du Palais, 1664.
———. *De la connoissance des bons livres ou examen de plusieurs autheurs.* Paris: A. Pralard, 1671.
———. *La Vraie Histoire comique de Francion.* Edited by Emile Colombey. Paris: Garnier, 1909.
TALLEMANT DES RÉAUX, GÉDÉON. *Historiettes.* Edited by Georges Mongrédien. Paris: Garnier, 1932-35.
TASSO, TORQUATO. *La Gerusalemme Liberata.* Firenze: Felice Le Monnier, 1853.
THIMM, CARL A. *A Complete Bibliography of Fencing and Duelling.* London and New York: John Lane, The Bodley Head, 1896.
THOMPSON, STITH. *Motif-Index of Folk-Literature.* Bloomington: Indiana University Press, 1955-58.
URFÉ, HONORÉ D'. *L'Astrée.* Première Partie. Edited by Hugues Vaganay. Lyon: Masson, 1925.
VEGA CARPIO, LOPE DE, FÉLIX. *El Peregrino en su patria.* In *Colección de las obras sueltas, assi en prosa, como en verso.* Tomo V. Madrid: Antonio de Sancha, 1776.
VILLEY, PIERRE. *Montaigne devant la postérité.* Paris: Boivin, 1935.
VIRGIL. *Aeneid.* Translated by H. Rush Fairclough for "Loeb Classical Library." London: Heinemann, 1918.
VOGLER, FREDERICK W. "D'Audiguier's *Le Pourtrait du Monde*: Two Centuries of Bibliographical Confusion", *Romance Notes,* III (1961-62), 29-32.
WALDBERG, MAX FREIHERR VON. *Der empfindsame Roman in Frankreich. Erster Teil: Die Anfänge bis zum Beginne des XVIII. Jahrhunderts.* Strassburg und Berlin: Trübner, 1906.
WILLIAMS, RALPH COPLESTONE. *Bibliography of the Seventeenth-Century Novel in France.* New York: The Century Co., 1931.
WINTER, CHARLES. "Audiguier (Vital d')." *Biographie universelle (Michaud) ancienne et moderne.* Paris: chez Mme C. Desplaces, 1854-65. II, 408f.
WURZBACH, WOLFGANG VON. *Geschichte des französischen Romans: 1. Band— Von den Anfängen bis zum Ende des XVII. Jahrhunderts.* Heidelberg: Carl Winter's Universitätsbuchhandlung, 1912.

www.ingramcontent.com/pod-product-compliance
Lightning Source LLC
Chambersburg PA
CBHW021844220426
43663CB00005B/393